Woke All Along

A Guidebook to Being Woke in Uncertain Times

SCOTT ROBINSON

ISBN 979-8302679840

Author photograph by Joshua Robinson

For Gretchen

Also by Scott Robinson ...

Humanizing: A Brief Guide to Humanism for the
        Interested but Non-Committal
Stand: A Handbook for Resisting Authoritarianism
Something to Think About: Pretty Big Questions about
        Pretty Important Things
The Indigenous Critique: On the Origin of Modern
        Democracy and the Truth about Western Culture

What's Next? The *West Wing* Guide to American Democracy
What's Next? The *West Wing* Guide to Global Politics

Table of Contents

Notes

Excerpts from the following previous books by the author have been included in chapters in this one:

*Chasing the Enterprise: Achieving Star Trek's
    Vision of the Human Future*
*The Children of Babel: Essays on the Inherent Nature
    of Artificial Intelligence and Consciousness*
Star Trek and Humanism
*Captain's Log: A Compendium of Thought, Opinion,
    and Analysis Concerning Star Trek*
*To Everything That Might Have Been:
    A Philosophical Journey Through Space: 1999*

Woke All Along

Introduction

Woke before 'Woke' was cool...

I'm a lifelong *Star Trek* fan, from its original incarnation through all the variations that have followed, and it is with great amusement that I observe today's fanboys griping about the overt social consciousness of the most recent ones.

"When did *Star Trek* get so Woke?" they complain – to the endless amusement of first-generation fans like myself. *Trek* has always been woke.

That's what attracted me to it. Its themes included diversity, equality, a commitment to truth, the eschewing of prejudice and bigotry – themes that I have taken deeply to heart.

Thus, these essays, each of which examines one of those themes. Am I Woke? Absolutely; I'd be ashamed *not* to be...

STR
December 2024

Diversity

Central to progressive values is the embrace of diversity, a virtue that sets many other virtues in motion. Humankind is naturally diverse, proliferating in endless variety. Taking delight in that diversity adds to the joy and mystery of living, and diffuses the bigotries around us. It's a natural starting point for the Woke journey.

Otherness vs. Sameness

The health and benefit of diversity might seem so obvious and essential that it might baffle those who embrace it that anyone would feel otherwise. But, of course, many do; on the flip side of diversity we find xenophobia – more recently rebranded *Othering*, the ancient tradition of lumping some people into a rejected or despised group apart from one's own.

Othering serves up mirror-image versions of diversity's categories: there is ethnic Othering, religious Othering, gender- or sex-based Othering. Political Othering, in particular, has made a spectacle of itself in recent years.

What is at the core of Othering?

"Othering is not about liking or disliking someone," wrote John A. Powell in *The Guardian*. "It is based on the conscious or unconscious assumption that a certain identified group poses a threat to the favoured group. It is largely driven by politicians and the media, as opposed to personal contact. Overwhelmingly, people don't "know" those that they are Othering."

It's that threat that drives otherness, wrote Čega se bojiš on Wordpress. "The fear of otherness is closely linked to the fear of the unknown and to the degree of trust in people. It is based on the fact that someone by their existence endangers what we consider 'our own' or 'ours.' It is often manifested in the form of fear that someone who has a different cultural characteristic to us – such as faith, language, customs and value system – endangers 'our' culture and way of life. According to this matrix, the influx of other people's elements into our cultural register leads to the long-term loss of 'our' identity and cultural affiliation.

"Otherness does not often come from far away. It is found in the neighbourhood, partly in the society and community to which we belong. Someone from a rival fan camp, someone on an opposing political-ideological spectrum, someone of extremely different material possibilities or understanding of sexual orientation and gender affiliation is a representative of the otherness which in the most radical forms often becomes a source of collective and individual fears."

In a 2016 interview by Jeffrey Goldberg in *The Atlantic*, then-President Barack Obama cited Othering as the primary source of most of the world's conflict: "tribe - us/them, a hostility toward the unfamiliar or unknown." It's not hard to see this reality reflected in even a cursory reading of human history; anywhere diversity has been lacking, Othering has flourished, to the detriment at all.

Progressives, whose focus is persistently fixed on a positive human future, understandably see Othering as a significant barrier to be addressed in progressing toward that future. The embrace and tireless nourishing of diversity everywhere is essential to tearing down that barrier.

The Progressive Stance on Diversity

The progressive commitment to diversity is included in its manifesto:

"Humanists are concerned for the well-being of all, are committed to diversity, and respect those of differing yet humane views. We work to uphold the equal enjoyment of human rights and civil liberties in an open, secular society and maintain it is a civic duty to participate in the democratic process and a planetary duty to protect nature's integrity, diversity, and beauty in a secure, sustainable manner."
(*Humanist Manifesto III*, 1993)

More than just a value statement, that commitment surfaces in the agendas of specific groups. There is a progressive Statement on Justice, Equity, Diversity, and Inclusion that says

"Pursuing justice, equity, diversity and inclusion is a moral imperative for the American Humanist Association (AHA), and integral to our work as advocates. Humanist values require the affirmation of the inherent dignity of every human being, as well as the related need to create a society where all can flourish and become one's best self." (American Humanist Association)

which is in turn operationalized by The Humanist Society as follows:

- We will foster and sustain an environment of inclusion, equity, and diversity through training, recruitment, and peer support.
- We will challenge long held opinions and assumptions and act in order to change them.
- We will evaluate and rectify organizational structures, policies, and practices that cause differential impact and limit access and opportunities for all chaplains, celebrants, and those they serve
- We will foster a culture of respect and inclusion that values the experiences and perspectives of all of our chaplains, celebrants, and those they serve
- We will address intergroup disparities in representation and retention through consistent dialogue and training, and intentional efforts to make our environment welcoming to individuals from underrepresented groups.
- We will support and advance a diverse collective and make intentional efforts to recruit individuals from underrepresented groups.
- We will provide resources and programs to promote individuals that enhance our ability to reach our goals of diversity, inclusion, and equity.

Humanism supports research in social science, including the *Journal of Humanistic Psychology*, which pursues "authentic humanistic research and scholarship, by definition, must reflect the vast diversity of human experiences, identities, and relationships (considering the whole person within contexts)."

So great is the progressive commitment to diversity that the global community of progressives itself is wildly diverse, making it notably distinct from other large groups, such as religions or political parties, which tend to possess far less diverse and far more like-minded constituents.

"Humanists are fairly diverse, as humanist ideas have arisen independently in many places at many different times," according to an essay on *Re:Online*. "There are humanist groups and organisations all over the world."

Consequently, "Humanists sometimes worry that humanism lacks a clear 'identity'. For the non-religious, it is not always easy to find a group identity, but many humanists are satisfied by their belief in human solidarity and/or the concept of 'multiple identities'..."

"If we all do the same thing every day, we don't grow, we don't evolve, we don't learn anything," said Rod Roddenberry, Gene Roddenberry's son, in an interview with *Variety*. "And so it is the diversity in everything, whether it's something outside, different trees, different looking people.

"We realized working together, we can do so much more. And so now we were trying to find people who looked at the universe in a different way, because we knew that we could grow and evolve by hearing something we'd never heard before. And whether we agreed with it or not, it was the hearing of that, the analyzing of it and the taking pieces out of it that we agreed with and incorporating into our own that allowed us to grow."

Racism and Social Inequality

Racism and social inequality have been with us for millennia, of course; even the holy texts of the major ancient religions are teeming with it. They are such a human constant that it's easy to assume that they are built into human nature.

But racism and social inequality are social phenomena, not natural phenomena. In this, he was showing his emerging progressive ideals, and humanism has much to say about these issues.

It can be safely said that there are no progressive organizations today that have not publicly renounced bigotry, racism, and other prejudicial behaviors, and to denounce instances of social inequality wherever they may be found.

Here are some examples:

"The principle of moral equality must be
furthered through elimination of all
discrimination based upon race, religion, sex, age,
or national origin. This means equality of
opportunity and recognition of talent and merit.
Individuals should be encouraged to contribute

to their own betterment. ... We deplore racial, religious, ethnic, or class antagonisms. Although we believe in cultural diversity and encourage racial and ethnic pride, we reject separations which promote alienation and set people and groups against each other; we envision an integrated community where people have a maximum opportunity for free and voluntary association.

"At the present juncture of history, commitment to all humankind is the highest commitment of which we are capable; it transcends the narrow allegiances of church, state, party, class, or race in moving toward a wider vision of human potentiality. What more daring a goal for humankind than for each person to become, in ideal as well as practice, a citizen of a world community."

~Eleventh Principle, Humanist Manifesto II

And this, from Humanists UK:

"Humanists condemn racism and racial discrimination in all its forms and are committed to campaigning for racial equality across all aspects of society. We have a positive track record throughout our existence in the fight for racial equality, from organising the first global race congress in 1911, to campaigning against colonialism in the early twentieth century, and for laws against racial discrimination from the mid-century. This commitment has continued through to today."

~Human Rights and Equality statement

And these excerpts from the Resolution on White Supremacy (American Humanist Association):

"*WHEREAS* white supremacy and the racism that sustains it remain particularized and systemic in our society, and

WHEREAS racism continues to limit the opportunities of and discriminate against racialized bodies of color in particular and marginalized bodies more generally, living in the United States by perpetuating inequality in every facet of individual and community life, and

WHEREAS hate crimes and hate groups have become more prevalent in the United States in recent years, especially targeting Black people, people perceived as Muslim, Jews, South Asians, LGBTQ people, and the disability community, and

WHEREAS dismantling white supremacy requires anti-racist action.

THEREFORE, BE IT RESOLVED that the AMERICAN HUMANIST ASSOCIATION, in the pursuit of an anti-racist society,

AFFIRMS that all lives will matter when Black lives

matter, and

AFFIRMS that economic justice for Black and Indigenous people requires federal policies that take drastic corrective measures to eradicate the racial wealth gap, and

AFFIRMS its support for anti-racist healthcare, including mental health services, that achieves the same health outcomes for Black and White people regardless of income, and

AFFIRMS its dedication to stamping out white supremacy and racism from within its organization through hiring practices, resource allocation, staff and board training, and more.

Per the progressive dynamic, it is of course not enough to take a political or philosophical position on racism; humanism calls for individual commitment and action. To that end, Samuel Kronen in "A Plea for a Humanist Antiracism" (in *Aero*, 2020) spells out some specifics:

> "A humanist antiracism would reject all racial double standards and express equal opprobrium at the police killings of both George Floyd and Tony Timpa. It would acknowledge the brutal legacy of historical racism, as well as the astounding racial progress made in the past half century, while never losing sight of how much further we have to go before race is irrelevant in public life. It would condemn racism in the

strongest possible terms and root out what remains of it in our institutions, without suggesting that racism is responsible for everything that's unfair in society. It would reject notions of intergenerational bloodguilt and retributive justice. It would strive for a race-blind world without ignoring instances of persistent racial injustice. It would create more breathing room for conversations about race, by allowing us to see each other as human beings and not simply as avatars of our races. It would appreciate the real advantages and disadvantages experienced by certain groups and individuals in society without making a religion out of the notion of privilege. It would reject the tendency to make meaning out of race and use race as a proxy for underlying social conditions. It would focus on hard policy reform over symbolic gestures of piety. It would measure progress by comparing metrics of well-being to those of the past rather than in terms of racial disparities. And it would reject systematic discrimination, whether in the form of overt racial quota systems in job applications and admissions procedures or subtle biases against blacks and other groups in policing, medicine and other sectors of American life."

Kronen's emphasis on social justice as the moving part in anti-racist action is echoed throughout the progressive communities and organizations of the world.

Here's what the AHA says about it:

> "Humanists are naturally committed to social justice as a prerequisite to peace and happiness for the greatest number and see it as a moral failing to stand by while others are denied their civil and human rights. Humanistic social justice advocacy involves respect for the equality of all people, compassion for their dignity and welfare, and a conviction that positive change requires human intervention.

> "The AHA takes an intersectional view of social justice issues, recognizing that working to liberate all marginalized communities is the best way to lift the prospects of any one group. Humanism motivates us to act on a moral imperative to transform systems of oppression because they are incompatible with the aspirations of humanism.

> "Regardless of race, ethnicity, economic status, ability, sexual orientation, gender identity, religious beliefs or nonbelief, or citizenship, all individuals have universal human rights that must be respected and protected. Achieving global standards for human rights and international adherence to institutions such as the International Criminal Court and the United Nations Universal Declaration of Human Rights

facilitate enforcing individuals' rights the world over."

Racism today

In the US today, racism and social inequality have been on the rise, as right-wing politicians stir the animosities of white America with divisive rhetoric. Systemic racism has existed throughout the nation's existence, and social/economic inequality was the persistent companion of that racism until the 1950s. The Civil Rights Movement produced some gains – there are now black millionaires, black CEOs, even a black president – and access to higher education is now much easier for members of all ethnicities.

But there is still far to go. In a recent study conducted by Harvard's T.H. Chan School of Public Health, 57% of black Americans reported discrimination in pay and eligibility for promotion; 54% of Native Americans reported facing discrimination in hiring, promotion, and compensation.

The National Urban League reported in its 2022 annual report that, per the Equality Index, black Americans are only getting 73% as much of the American pie as white Americans; a black child born today can expect a life four years shorter, on average, than a white child; black women are 59% more likely to die while bearing a child than white women; 31% are more likely to die of breast cancer; black men are 52% more likely to die of prostate cancer.

According to a 2019 study by the Pew Research Center, 58% of Americans believe that racism in the nation is serious, and 56% believe that the Trump presidency made it worse. 51% of Americans believe that being Hispanic hinders a person's ability to succeed in the US. Among blacks themselves, 78% do not think enough has been done to address systemic racism in the US.

Regarding the expression of racist opinions and insensitive views, 65% of Americans believe that expression became more common after Donald Trump became president; 45% said it has become more acceptable.

Among white Democrats, 64% say they do not believe the nation has done enough to address systemic racism; among white Republicans, the number is 15%. 80% of white Democrats say the legacy of slavery continues to impact American society today, while only 40% of white Republicans feel the same. And 78% of white Democrats say the problem is people not seeing racism where it exists, while the same percentage of white Republicans say that people see racial discrimination where it really isn't.

How we get Woke

Humanities Professor Anthony Pinn of Rice University[1] gets more specific still, offering a list of Dos and Don'ts for the individual progressive to apply when actively confronting racism:

- **Don't make blanket statements concerning African-American involvement in theism.**

"The relationship between African-Americans and Christianity is complex and layered," Pinn points out; in the African-American past, it pushed against injustice and helped produce a sense of identity and agency that worked against the dehumanization they were experiencing.

- **Don't assume humanism is a vaccine against poor thinking and poor behavior.** Humanists, Pinn asserts, are cultural creatures, and can be insensitive to racial injustice through the simple mechanism of believing that the logic they embrace elevates them beyond it.

- **Don't assume you get to set the racial justice agenda.** "You don't get to determine what are appropriate markers of progress," Pinn writes; "your job is to promote solidarity, and to play the role assigned to you by those who are most directly and deeply impacted by issues of race and racism."

- **Do recognize the nature of privilege.** "Whiteness" comes with perks, Pinn states. There are forms of privilege that lurk in the background, to which the humanist should be alert: the assumption that the police are there to serve and protect, for instance, and the assumption that you weren't placed near the restroom in the restaurant because of the color of your skin.

- **Do educate yourself.** The serious progressive should put the same energy into learning about matters of race, Pinn insists, that they put toward learning about separation of church and state, evolution, and other important progressive issues.

- **Do recognize difference as an opportunity.** Difference, per Pinn, is "an opportunity... a chance to add complexity to a community and to learn from approaches and perspectives outside what is considered normative. It's an opportunity to appreciate what has been considered marginal to U.S. life and to understand its actual centrality. In a certain way, difference as opportunity points to the need to appreciate cultural diversity, learn from it, and embrace possibilities that push us beyond the familiar and comfortable."

All pretty Woke, isn't it?

Rights and Freedoms

Most of the pushback against Woke is about rights – human rights, civil rights, political rights, economic rights, social rights, cultural rights. If you're Woke, you generally believe that these rights, and the freedoms they enshrine, should be available to all; if you're not Woke, you generally believe that some people should have fewer rights than others.

The tendency of the anti-Woke to attack some specific groups – LGBTQ, for instance – is examined below. But the general pushback against equal rights for all exists over and above specific attacks on specific groups; it is founded on a belief, held by far too many, that some people are better or more worthy than others.

That belief flies in the face of democracy, of course; but the staggering depth of the chasm between the Woke view on rights and freedoms and the view of Woke's opposition is truly commitment to two separate realities.

"The basic tool for the manipulation of reality is the manipulation of words. If you can control the meaning of words, you can control the people who must use the words." ~Philip K. Dick

The dual realities we find ourselves confronting is based on two completely different meanings of the word *freedom*.

The point of rights is to secure freedoms; attacks on the rights of any particular group are an attempt to restrict or remove that group's freedoms. Defense of those rights, conversely, are attempts to preserve those freedoms.

What freedoms are we talking about?

If you're Woke, those include freedom from persecution over sexual orientation, gender identity, skin color or ethnicity. You support equal rights for persons in these groups, and expect the government to enforce those rights. 'We the People', to you, means people of all colors, ethnic origins, religions, and sexual persuasions.

If you aren't, *freedom* doesn't mean rights shared by all, enforced by the government; it means freedom *from* government.

This idea has been in the US water supply for more than a century, but it took root in the public gestalt with the election of Ronald Reagan to the White House in 1980. It was a coup for a particular cabal of economists, politicians, and businessmen – disciples of *neoliberalism*.

Neoliberalism and freedom

The neoliberal agenda is vast, but its central tenets are easily summarized:

- The US government is your enemy;
- The government needs to get out of the business of helping average Americans;
- The well-being of business transcends the national interest;
- *Deregulate, deregulate, deregulate!*

Ronald Reagan was a neoliberal juggernaut on all these fronts, setting the tone and strategy for all in the GOP who would follow him.

His assaults on the democratic order weren't just systematic and persistent; they were overt, out in the open, often paraded on national television.

"Government is not the solution to our problem, government *is* the problem," he declared, followed later by, "The nine most terrifying words in the English language are: 'I'm from the government, and I'm here to help.'" – casually vilifying, at a stroke, the hundreds of thousands who *do* enter public service out of a deep desire and conviction to help others and contribute to the betterment of the nation.

Reagan's demonization of government, already a GOP staple, was perhaps the least of it; his valentine to capitalism, a gutting of tax policy that had been in place since World War II, requiring businesses and the very wealthy to contribute their fair share back to the economy that had enriched them, exploded the national debt. In cutting the top tax rate from 70% to 25%, he tripled that debt, from $738 billion to $2.4 trillion. That quickly, the US went from being the world's largest creditor to the world's largest debtor.

The justification was that the US economy wasn't functioning properly, but that wasn't true at all. The economy had boomed steadily during the post-World War II years, with only the normal fluctuations. The number of people in the US living in poverty had continually declined, even as the overall population rose.

In the process, Reagan and his allies laid track for the GOP to come by dissembling in the media to justify his agenda. His budget director, David Stockman, perpetuated the trickle-down gospel that cutting taxes on corporations and the wealthy would trigger large returns as the savings would be re-invested in the economy, in effect paying for the cuts. The Office of Management and Budget debunked this myth with actual analysis, prompting Stockman to confess publicly that "None of us really understands what's going on with all these numbers... the whole thing is premised on faith, on a belief about how the world works."

'Trickle-down' wasn't real economic theory; it was conservative, neoliberal ideology. And when Stockman later said publicly that the tax cuts really were, in fact, a valentine to business, calling the whole thing a 'Trojan horse', he was castigated by the president.

Forty years later, 'trickle-down' has yet to function as promised, even though the current crop of GOP politicians continue to shop it; the money the uber-wealthy are saving on their tax bills isn't and never has been re-invested in the economy. It sits in off-shore accounts.

A firestorm of deregulation followed the tax cuts, stagnating the prosperity of the middle class as the growth of the minimum wage dropped away and economic inequality surged. The push for privatization of government began in earnest, sending healthcare costs into the stratosphere, and barriers to the exporting of US manufacturing to nations where labor was far cheaper evaporated. The export of US manufacturing to other countries, gutting the domestic jobs market as it dismantled unions, was accompanied by a breathtaking surge in the trade deficit. Reagan inherited from Carter a deficit of only $13 billion; when he left office, it had soared to a mind-blowing $685 billion.

Perhaps most damning was the elimination of the Fairness Doctrine in 1987. The policy that had protected the integrity of public information since the dawn of radio was dropped, enabling the wild-west, anything-goes parade of disinformation and outright deception that clogs up media today. The airwaves ceased to be conduits for news and became what they are today – ideology pipelines.

Neoliberalism was off and running. The global, regulation-free landscape for the cultivation of wealth envisioned by Milton Friedman and his cohorts was finally taking shape. The transformation of the US government from the middle-class-building, consumer-protecting, civil-rights-promoting agency it had become since the New Deal into capitalism's passive enabler was well underway.

Reaganism was indeed a Trojan horse, and the forces

it unleashed have ended or endangered many of the institutions we thought would last forever. Civil discourse in the conducting of the people's business is long gone; inequality has surged; people no longer trust those they count on to protect them. Deceit has been normalized, the rule of law is precarious, and violence – even murder! – in pursuit of political ends is becoming acceptable on US soil.

All so Elon Musk can go to Mars.

Born in the South

Historian Heather Cox Richardson reminds us that this way of thinking goes back to the Civil War: the precursor to modern neoliberalism was the slave trade of the 19th century South, and the wealthy men who enabled it:[1]

"The Thirteenth Amendment abolished human enslavement in the United States, except as punishment for a crime (an exception that later enabled the use of chain gangs). President Abraham Lincoln and the congressmen who embraced this monumental change to the Constitution expected that ending enslavement would end the power of a few elite southerners to dismantle the United States.

"Enslavement, they believed, had enabled a few men to monopolize wealth and power in the American South, where they dominated state governments and wrote laws to protect their own interests. Those same men had taken over first the Democratic Party and then the national government, controlling the Supreme Court, the Senate, and the presidency.

"The elite southerners insisted that the national government had no power to do anything that was not spelled out in the Constitution. It could protect the property interests of enslavers - through a law forcing free states to return escaped slaves, for example, or laws protecting enslavement in the western territories - but it could not do anything to help ordinary Americans, like dredging harbors, building roads, or establishing colleges, no matter how popular those measures might be.

"During the Civil War, Lincoln and his party rejected this old formula and created a new one. They pioneered a government that responded to the interests of ordinary Americans. Amending the Constitution to end enslavement was not simply an attempt to guarantee freedom for Black Americans; it was also designed to cement in place the government 'of the people, by the people, for the people.'

"Demonstrating that momentous change, the second section of the Thirteenth Amendment added: 'Congress shall have power to enforce this article by appropriate legislation.' The first ten amendments to the Constitution - the Bill of Rights - limited the power of the federal government. The Thirteenth was the first to expand it.

"[Lincoln and his supporters] knew that Black southerners supported this new government. They believed that poorer white southerners who had been crushed economically before the war as wealthy white enslavers gobbled up the region's best land and who had borne the brunt of the war would also embrace it. Under the new system, the North had defied all expectations and thrived during the war, and they thought its superiority to the old system was so obvious that ordinary southerners would jump at it.

"Many did... but white lawmakers in the southern states did not. They agreed to ratify the Thirteenth Amendment, but enabled by President Andrew Johnson, who took over the presidency after Lincoln's assassination, they passed a series of laws that bound Black Americans to yearlong contracts working in white-owned fields, prohibited Black Americans from meeting together or owning guns, demanded that Black Americans behave submissively to white Americans, and sometimes punished white people who interacted with their Black neighbors.

"The *Chicago Tribune* wrote, 'The men of the North will turn the State of Mississippi into a frog-pond before they will allow any such laws to disgrace one foot of soil in which the bones of our soldiers sleep and over which the flag of freedom waves.' To counter these 'Black Codes,' Congress wrote the Fourteenth Amendment in 1866, and the states ratified it in 1868.

"Congress designed the Fourteenth Amendment to end forever the ability of state lawmakers to undermine the United States of America. The amendment declared anyone born or naturalized in the United States to be a U.S. citizen and then established the power of the federal government to stop states from discriminating against citizens. The Fourteenth Amendment establishes that states must treat everyone equally before the law, and they can't take away someone's rights without due process of the law."

The Civil War, then, provides us with a mirror in which to view our situation today: to the Woke North, *freedom* meant *freedom for both white and black*; to the anti-Woke South (the wealthy slaveowners, anyway), *freedom* meant *freedom from the federal government's interference in our right to take away the freedom of black people.*

'Twas ever thus. The Woke struggle is just another expression of a conflict that has burdened humankind since the invention of the idea of property: some believe they are more equal than others – and the wealthy, in particular, have been the ones to seize power whenever possible to secure their wealth by trimming away the power, rights, and freedoms of those others.

Operation Iraqi Freedom?

In another modern example, part of the Right's rhetoric over the conquest of Iraq in 2003 was that the invasion would democratize that nation – restore *freedom* to the Iraqi people. When President George Bush announced the invasion on March 19, 2003, he put a name to it: Operation Iraqi Freedom.

It's hard to imagine a greater irony, even from him.

"A peaceful world of growing freedom," Bush wrote on the first anniversary of 9/11, "serves American long-term interests, reflects enduring American ideals and unites America's allies. Humanity holds in its hands the opportunity to offer freedom's triumph over all its age-old foes... as the greatest power on Earth, we have an obligation to help the spread of freedom."

Reading those words, the average American would assume Bush meant we were invading Iraq to spread equal rights, to ensure the freedoms of all its citizens, regardless of their religion, color, sexual orientation, and so on. Like in America.

But, no; the *freedom* we were spreading was *neoliberalism*.

In September of the same year, Paul Bremer, head of the Coalition Provisional Authority, produced a series of orders to be implemented in the new Iraq:

- The full privatization of public enterprises;
- Full ownership rights, by foreign firms, of Iraqi businesses;
- The opening of Iraq's banks to foreign control;
- The elimination of all trade barriers.

Put another way, Iraq was to be *deregulated*.

On the other hand, what *would* be regulated – and heavily so - would be Iraqi workers themselves:

- Strikes were effectively forbidden in key sectors;
- The right to unionize was heavily restricted;
- A regressive flat tax would be imposed.

Iraqi was not to be made a *free* state in the sense that most Americans understand the term; it was to be made a *neoliberal* state, one that existed under conditions friendly to neoliberal visions of global markets.

When we wrap our heads around this appropriation of words and the imposition of very different meanings, we more clearly understand the staggering distance between Woke thought and convictions, and the thought and convictions of those who oppose it.

Governance as incentive

Conservatives, and neoliberals in particular, want to shrink government to the point they can drown it because they believe government is only good for one thing: protecting their property. All its other functions, particularly social functions, should be eradicated.

As they say that, they profess to be all for human flourishing, but that the *market* should be the source of that flourishing – not government.

The problem is, when people are flourishing, the wealthy can be counted on to find a way to exploit them. And the market can't do anything to stop them. Government is necessary to incentivize the proliferation of the freedoms that improve human well-being, because the market certainly doesn't; and, conversely, the government is necessary to *dis*-incentivize exploitation and the violation of the rights of others, by punishing those violations.

Other forces for Woke

We can imagine that the United Federation of Planets has a universal manifesto articulating the rights and freedoms of its citizens, and that these are enshrined somewhere for all to see. We have some similar codifications of our own.

The United Nations Universal Declaration on Human Rights

"Human rights include the right to life and liberty, freedom from slavery and torture, freedom of opinion and expression, the right to work and education, and many more. Everyone is entitled to these rights, without discrimination."

The UN specifies 30 basic human rights:

- All human beings are free and equal
- No discrimination
- Right to life
- No slavery
- No torture and inhuman treatment
- Same right to use law
- Equal before the law
- Right to treated fair by court
- No unfair detainment
- Right to trial
- Innocent until proved guilty
- Right to privacy
- Freedom to movement and residence
- Right to asylum
- Right to nationality
- Rights to marry and have family
- Right to own things
- Freedom of thought and religion
- Freedom of opinion and expression
- Right to democracy
- Right to social security
- Right to work
- Right to rest and holiday
- Right of social service
- Right to education
- Right of cultural and art

- Freedom around the world
- Subject to law
- Human rights can't be taken away

The International Covenant on Economic, Social, and Cultural Rights (1976)

The human rights that the Covenant seeks to promote and protect include:

- the right to work in just and favourable conditions;
- the right to social protection, to an adequate standard of living and to the highest attainable standards of physical and mental well-being;
- the right to education and the enjoyment of benefits of cultural freedom and scientific progress.

Freedom House

"Democracy depends on the guarantee of equal rights under law and freedom from discrimination for all individuals in a society. If the rights and freedoms of one segment of the population are violated with impunity, the same sorts of abuses are likely to be visited on others. Those forced to endure a subordinate status have less incentive to play by the rules, creating a vicious circle of defiance and repression."

Woke knows where it stands, when it comes to rights. Freedoms.

LGBTQ

In the Right's War on Woke, there are few issues as venomous as sexual orientation. People who don't conform to a white, Christian view of the bedroom seem to make them disturbingly uncomfortable.

This is no surprise. Long before the word "woke" came along – long before "conservative" and "liberal" became sociopolitical designations – authoritarian and patriarchal personalities have bristled and howled over people who do not conform to their notions of correct and proper sexuality. We don't have to look further than the Old Testament to realize this way of thinking has been with us for thousands of years.

This does not fully explain, however, the anti-Woke crowd's laser-sharp targeting of LGBTQ people at this particular moment in history. So intense has these attacks become that they echo the Right's war on the environment: they despise pro-LGBTQ policy so deeply that they vigorously assault businesses who deploy it – even though the pro-LGBTQ policies are good for business, and (on paper) they themselves are pro-business.

Here are some examples:

- Per a report in *Forbes*, when Woolworths

tweeted support for International Pride Month, expressing commitment to their LGBTQ customers, conservative outrage ensued; Woolworth's doubled down, tweeting that "every person has the right to dignity, regardless of their identity; this is a fact enshrined in our constitution, it is not up for debate";

- Similar conservative outrage erupted in New Zealand, when The Warehouse retail outlet sold items from the Disney pride collection;
- More of the outrage emerged over *Glamour UK*, which featured a picture of pregnant transgender man Logan Broan on its cover;
- According to the *Dallas Morning News*, Southwest Airlines has been forced to deal with a website and local billboard smearing it as "Southwoke" for its promotion of racial and LGBTQ diversity;
- Target bowed to similar anti-Woke pressure, pulling LGBTQ items from its Pride collection when workers' safety was threatened, according to the *Washington Post*;
- The *New York Times* reported that Anheuser-Busch made a similar retreat in the face of conservative boycotts following TikTok star Dylan Mulvaney's promotion of a beer contest; two of the company's top executives were put on leave, and the company announced that its future marketing would focus on sports and music.

"Recent pushback against businesses such as Anheuser-Busch and Target, blatantly organized by extremist groups, serves as a wake up call for all businesses that support the LGBTQ+ community," read a statement from the Human Rights Campaign. "We've seen this extremist playbook of attacks before. Their goal is clear: to prevent LGBTQ+ inclusion and representation, silence our allies and make our community invisible."

As with the rage over businesses treating the environment responsibly, this behavior makes no economic sense: the asset management group LGBT Capital estimates that the annual purchasing power of the global LGBTQ community is $3.9 trillion. No business in its right mind would turn its back on such a broad customer base.

It's not just the assault on business; worse than that is the assault on law.

The Republican governor of Florida, Ron DeSantos, has become the public face of the anti-LGBTQ Right, with two major bills that have received national attention and scrutiny: an "anti-woke" bill and the "Don't Say Gay" bill. Both are designed to dictate what teachers can and cannot say in classrooms. The first presents a list of race-related concepts that are forbidden in lessons for students; the second prohibits discussion of sexual orientation and gender identity in grade school classrooms. The irony in the latter case, of course, is that teachers were not presenting those topics to children of that age in the first place, suggesting that the law is pure political posturing.

At the federal level, anti-LGBTQ legislation has been surfacing in must-pass funding bills in the House of Representatives, with Republican lawmakers embedding 45 such provision in those bills in an attempt to weaken discrimination protections for same-sex couples and restrict gender-affirming care. Several appropriations bills include provisions for the restriction of gender transition care for those on Medicare, Medicaid, and ACA-subsidized plans. They would also impact trans members of the military and their dependents, as well as federal employees. There are also provisions for the banning of Pride flags over government buildings, the nullification of protections for same-sex couples, and restriction of funding of programs promoting diversity and inclusion.

Down in Texas, the Republican Party has formally defined homosexuality as an "abnormal lifestyle choice" and openly stated its opposition to "all efforts to validate transgender identity." The party platform includes a call to repeal the 1965 Voting Rights Act, as well as a statement that LGBTQ people should not be legally protected from discrimination. It further states that being gay or trans is a choice.

"We believe there should be no granting of special legal entitlements or creation of special status for homosexual behavior, regardless of state of origin, and we oppose any criminal or civil penalties against those who oppose homosexuality out of faith, conviction, or belief in traditional values," it reads.

Texas Republicans have also called for a ban on gender-affirming care.

In 2022, more than 300 anti-LGBTQ bills were pending in state legislatures. According to the Human Rights Campaign, at least six states have banned transgender women and girls from competing on sports teams consistent with their gender. Alabama, Arizona and Texas have taken steps to ban gender-affirming care for young people; in Alabama, it is now a felony for a doctor to provide such care to minors. Other states are also following Florida's lead, introducing bills that mimic "Don't Say Gay".

Three states now have laws in place preventing trans children from accessing care for gender dysphoria, even when recommended by major medical associations. Two have outlawed discussion of LGBTQ history or individuals in classrooms.

And then there are the Christians...

Randall Balmer, a professor at Dartmouth who grew up in an Evangelical household, offers some perspective on the breathtaking surge in LGBTQ hatred, noting that much of it comes from Evangelicals. The point of it all, he has written, is to keep that community mobilized as a voting block for the Right.[1]

"They have an interest in keeping the base riled up about one thing or another, and when one issue fades, as with same-sex relationships and same-sex marriage, they've got to find something else," Balmer said in an interview with *The 19th*. "It's almost frantic."

His research traces this methodology to Paul Weyrich, one of the founders of the Religious Right, in the Seventies. Weyrich began testing issues that would drive Evangelicals to the voting booth, and this became a standard practice, permanently installing white Evangelicals as the key factor in Republican wins.

Once gay marriage was settled, much to the Religious Right's chagrin, "they almost frantically began looking for something else," Balmer said. "And of course, the trans thing was the next thing on the horizon."

What the public thinks

What does the general public think of all this? Unsurprisingly, there's a clear partisan divergence: 3/4ths of Republicans say the US should promote traditional values, and two-thirds of Democrats support greater tolerance of diversity. Independents are split down the middle.

That poll gets more granular, asking very specific questions about tolerance from a public policy viewpoint:

- Government should promote greater respect for traditional values: 27% (D), 65% (R)
- Government should promote greater tolerance of people with different lifestyles: 66% (D), 18% (R)
- US should increase social justice: 66% (D), 21% (R)
- The country should reduce political correctness and cancel culture: 19% (D), 67% (R)
- Promotion of LGBTQ lifestyle and values has

gone too far: 12% (D), 70% (R)
- The US should be more accepting of the LGBTQ community: 60% (D), 10% (R)

US voters across the political spectrum acknowledge that the surge in anti-LGBTQ legislation is political theater more than moral conviction. In a 2023 Data for Progress survey, those who think there is "too much" legislation aimed at "limiting the rights of transgender and gay people in America" include 64% of voters in general; 72% of Democrats, 65% of Independents, and 55% of Republicans.

General support for marriage equality is now around 70%, with PRRI's 2022 American Values Atlas noting that same-sex marriage support is at 60% or greater in 43 states.

Per the non-partisan Public Religion Research Institute, almost 80% of Americans support protections against discrimination for LGBTQ people (this even includes 65% of Republicans). A 2021 PBS Newshour/NPR/Marist poll reported that 2/3[rd]s of Americans oppose bills that limit transgender rights.

We've already noted in the broader discussion of diversity above that our differences make human community stronger. Increasing diversity and tolerance, and pushing back against attacks on both, is not only noble; it's a means of improving our collective capability and accelerating human progress. It is worthy of our deep commitment and investment.

The past few decades of American life have

demonstrated what honest, self-aware people have known all along: skin color makes no difference; gender makes no difference. And neither does sexual orientation. It's as Woke to support the LGBTQ community as it is to support racial and gender equality.

Authoritarianism

The War on Woke is essentially an Authoritarian war on non-Authoritarian values. Conversely, the values embraced by those considered Woke are egalitarian – anti-authoritarian – values. This isn't the only framing we can apply to the Woke conflict, but it's by far the most substantial.

Authoritarianism, then, is an essential issue to be considered when viewing Woke thought through the *Star Trek* lens.

Alpha males

In most primate cultures, the alpha male rules.

A single individual, more powerful than his peers, governs the group by means of strength and intimidation, and in the process inculcates fear in others, takes females at will, and enjoys the highest level of privilege – until toppled from power by a superior challenger. So the story goes, among apes and throughout human history.

The assumption is that we naturally conform to this 'alpha' framework of authority.

But if we are more bonobo than chimpanzee, it no longer makes sense; and if we truly are off course, socially – having
screwed up millennia of cooperative social order when we ceased to be migratory – then the idea of alpha humans no longer makes sense.

This is what we're talking about when we invoke the term *authoritarianism*. It is used in both political science (to describe the political orientation of a nation-state) and psychology (to describe the dynamics of leader-and-follower, where authoritarianism is the rule). It does not differ significantly, in social terms, from what we observe in chimpanzees.

And when it took hold of humankind, it took hold big: for many thousands of years, our sociopolitical systems have been far more authoritarian than not.

Authoritarianism strips the individual of self-determination. By centralizing authority in an individual, it strips the group of the benefit of pooled knowledge and decision-making skills. By awarding group rule according to personal power, rather than according to actual leadership merits, it represents a danger to the group that amplifies over time.

The authoritarian regimes that have come and gone over the millennia that human beings have been civilized are countless. Even in the modern era, the age of democracy, authoritarianism continues to rise up, threatening to return us to a sociopolitically captive state.

This couldn't have happened in the Paleolithic. Human survival hinged on multiple axes, not just one: the group required the leadership of a long-term planner, able to anticipate environmental conditions and food supplies months in advance; adept pattern-finders were needed, individuals able to sense weather change and changes in the behavior of prey; and fast-response captains were needed, in moments of sudden attack from predators.

That's not a single leader – that's several, each with a different skill set…a different cognitive style.

Among chimpanzees, authoritarian leadership limits the tribe; it is not able to organize beyond swarming on prey and

internal power struggle. It is a constant competition for the top spot, with no attention to the social development of the tribe.

Among the bonobos, leadership is distributed, as it is in democracies. No one individual member of the tribe holds absolute power, and anyone who tries is rapidly slapped down.

Put simply: when we enabled authoritarianism, we were stepping backward, not forward – and we created a danger that threatens us today, possibly more than it ever has before.

What the expert says

The pacesetter in the academic study of authoritarianism is Bob Altemeyer, retired professor of psychology at the University of Manitoba. The most aggressive investigator of authoritarianism for more than three decades, Altemeyer's books on the subject are essential reading for any who would undertake its study.

Long established in academic circles, Altemeyer came

to national attention when his explanation of authoritarian behaviors in American politics made their way into the polemics of John Dean (of Watergate fame). At Dean's urging, Altemeyer wrote a book on the subject for laypeople.[1]

Altemeyer has, not surprisingly, had a great deal to say about Donald Trump.

"Authoritarian followers in America today are tremendously energized by fear and anger," he wrote in March 2016. "They're scared, and they want someone really strong and confident to protect them. It's a very natural, understandable reaction.

"Wanna-be tyrants in a democracy are just comical figures on soapboxes when they have no following. So the real threat lay coiled in parts of the population itself, it was thought, ready someday to catapult the next Hitler to power with their votes."

His explanation of the thinking of authoritarian followers illuminates their choice of Donald Trump:

"Research suggests that 20-25% of the adults in North America are highly vulnerable to a demagogue who would incite hatred of various minorities to gain power. These people
are waiting for a tough "man on horseback" who will supposedly solve all our problems through the ruthless application of force. When such a man gains prominence, you can expect the authoritarian followers to mate devotedly with the authoritarian leader, because each gives the other something they desperately want: the feeling of safety for the followers, and the tremendous power of the modern state for the leader.

Not all Trump voters qualify as authoritarian

followers, Altemeyer wrote, "but they likely compose his hard-core base. Furthermore, many authoritarian followers [supported] Senator Ted Cruz for religious reasons." He went on to predict "most of them [will] slide into the Trump ranks once Cruz drops out of the race. By summer [2016], the vast majority of authoritarian followers in the United States will likely be for Trump."

Which, of course, is exactly what happened.

As for what happens next, "If you believe that a President Trump would be a very stiff test of democracy in the United States, then what can you do?... Well, it's not going to be easy changing highly aggressive, dogmatic, insular people who will dismiss you out of hand as the enemy... they have been that way for most of their lives, and they have built a lot of supports, including straight-out denial, to keep their views intact.

"One suspects they will feel even more betrayed if... [Trump] turns out to have been conning them all along, too. But he is going to keep telling them he's one of them, and keep them scared and angry while selling himself as the Toughest Guy They Ever Met. Authoritarian followers are always waiting for The Leader, and now they firmly believe they've found him."

Here's a list of traits Altemeyer observes in authoritarian followers:

1. They are highly ethnocentric, highly inclined to see the world as their in-group versus everyone else. Because they are so committed to their in-group, they are very zealous in its cause.

2. They are highly fearful of a dangerous world. Their parents taught them, more than parents usually do, that the world is dangerous. They may also be genetically predisposed to experiencing stronger fear than most people do.

3. They are highly self-righteous. They believe they are the "good people" and this unlocks a lot of hostile impulses against those they consider bad.

4. They are aggressive. Given the chance to attack someone with the approval of an authority, they will lower the boom.

5. They are highly prejudiced against racial and ethnic minorities, non-heterosexuals, and women in general.

6. Their beliefs are a mass of contradictions. They have highly compartmentalized minds, in which opposite beliefs exist side-by-side in adjacent boxes. As a result, their thinking is full of double standards.

7. They reason poorly. If they like the conclusion of an argument, they don't pay much attention to whether the evidence is valid or the argument is consistent.

8. They are highly dogmatic. Because they have gotten their beliefs mainly from the authorities in their lives, rather than think things out for themselves, they have no real defense when facts or events indicate they are wrong. So they just dig in their heels and refuse to change.

9. They are very dependent on social reinforcement of their beliefs. They think they are right because almost everyone they know, almost every news broadcast they see, almost every radio commentator
they listen to, tells them they are. That is, they screen out the sources that will suggest that they are wrong.
10. Because they severely limit their exposure to different people and ideas, they vastly overestimate the extent to which other people agree with them.
11. And thinking they are "the moral majority" supports their attacks on the "evil minorities" they see in the country.
12. They are easily duped by manipulators who pretend to espouse their causes when all the con artists really want is personal gain.
13. They are largely blind to themselves. They have little self-understanding and insight into why they think and do what they do.

Altemeyer's Global Change Game

Altemeyer writes of some experiments he conducted with a team in 1994. They involved the Global Change Game, a simulation of international-level interactions between groups of students, meant to explore issues affecting the planet and humankind as a whole.

The game is played on a map the size of a basketball court. A group of 70 students or so play the game together, each assigned to one of 10 regions of the world, representing 100 million people. Assets are distributed among the regions, and each has its own set of issues to deal with: health, hunger, deforestation, climate change, energy shortages, encroaching desert, economic instability, international trade, inequality – all of these and more can appear on the horizon of any world region.

Three of the regions are nuclear superpowers. Conventional military power is distributed as it is in the real world, and several start off the game with indigenous poverty – again, as in the real world. Facilitators (faculty members) present each region with problems, and it is left to the teams in each region to reach out to request or offer aid, to enter into alliances, to band together to solve problems or oppose one another and create new ones.

Several of the students declare themselves "Elites" – leaders – and the game allows for such players to squirrel away some of their region's wealth for themselves.

Regions can enter into trade agreements, take in refugees, pollute the oceans, offer humanitarian aid, screw up the world economy, and even declare nuclear war (which ends the game by default). After 40 simulated years of international activity, the game is declared over, and points are tallied to determine the winning region.

The Low-Authoritarians. Altemeyer's innovation was to populate one night's run of the game purely with students who had scored low on his RWA scale –

students low in Authoritarianism (the students were not made aware that their RWA scores had anything to do with the game). These students managed to achieve world peace and international cooperation. The 10 Elites (seven men, three women) joined together on Tasmania whenever a crisis arose and solved the problem together.

The three nuclear superpowers chose to disarm, and no war broke out during the playing of the game. An ozone depletion crisis announced by the facilitators was solved with the combined economic support of the wealthiest nations and advanced technology. There were several hundred million deaths resulting from disease and starvation in poverty-stricken countries (Europe sent aid – North America refused). World population at the end of the game was 8.7 billion, but resources were distributed worldwide in such a way as to support almost all of them. Overall, Altemeyer considered it a great success.

The High-Authoritarians. The following night, the game was repeated – this time with students who had all scored high on the Authoritarian scale. The Elites (all male) declined to disarm, and instead began heavy militarization. The Middle East region immediately doubled oil prices. The Soviet Union prepared to invade North America. A nuclear exchange followed soon after, ending the game.

The facilitators turned off the lights and described the effects of nuclear winter to the students before restarting the game. This time, the Soviet Union invaded China, killing 400 million. The Elite from the Middle East called a United Nations meeting, but nothing came of it.

The ozone depletion crisis occurred, but no cooperative activity was attempted. The European region made some independent efforts to reduce emissions, but the problem got steadily worse. Poverty and population growth went unchecked around the world. Rather than address their nation's economic challenges, the Elites maneuvered for personal power. Alliances were formed, with stronger partners forcing weaker ones to buy in.

At the end of 40 simulated years, the planet was coming apart, facing mounting crises, armed to the teeth and ready for holocaust. A total of 1,700 million people were dead. The Elites had plundered their regions for personal wealth.

And these were college students!

"There they were, in a big room full of people *just like themselves*, and they all turned their backs on each other and paid attention only to their own group," Altemeyer wrote later. "They too were all reading from the same page, but write large on their page was, 'Care About Your Own; We Are NOT All In This Together'."

The implications of these experiments are staggering. These two groups of students varied *only* in their test scores on the Right-Wing Authoritarian Scale; in every other way, they were
typical college students, ages 18-22, predominantly white, middle-class, with age-appropriate concerns.

Yet when faced with the opportunity to cooperate or enter into conflict, their differing levels of Authoritarianism caused them to behave entirely differently.

Think about that for a moment. If that can happen in

two evenings of game play among young people, it is no surprise to see what we see in the world around us today and throughout history, when power is placed in the hands of adults with these same tendencies and impulses.

Altemeyer and the authoritarian mind

Most of the contents of the Authoritarian mind have come under Altemeyer's scrutiny. In his dozens of studies over the years, he has made use of many instruments, measuring everything from ethnocentricity to dogmatism to logical fallacy. The collective result is a remarkably sharp image of that mind, one that will be familiar to anyone who has that belligerent Fox News-watching uncle who can't shut up about what he heard yesterday on talk radio.

Altemeyer isn't the only one. A number of social scientists have conducted studies investigating the personality features that seem to define Authoritarians. They collectively form a cognitive portrait that is both familiar and remarkably consistent.

Prejudice and bigotry

Altemeyer developed an instrument for measuring an individual's level of ethnocentrism, the Manitoba Ethnocentrism Scale. Subjects rate the truth or falsehood of statements about members of other ethnicities on a scale of -4 to +4, yielding an index of ethnocentric orientation that can be correlated with results on other instruments, such as his RWA scale. In repeated experiments in both Canada and the United States, subjects who scored high on one strongly tended to score high on the other.

He noted that Authoritarian followers who were prejudiced against one ethnic group tended to be prejudiced toward them all – and toward other out-groups, such as homosexuals, as well (this finding has long been established by social psychologists). "Authoritarian followers dislike so many kinds of people, I have called them 'equal opportunity bigots'."

As mentioned in the chapter "A Sociopolitical Family Portrait", Authoritarians are often religious fundamentalists. It's an identity marker, Altemeyer noted, and that reinforced the Authoritarian Us, as noted in the chapter "Authoritarian 'Us' v. Egalitarian 'Them'". He put all of this together in yet another instrument, the Religious Ethnocentrism Scale.

The scale measures the degree to which the subject feels their religion should be the national religion; the degree to which other religions should be ignored; the undesirability of mixing with those with differing beliefs, and so on. For good measure, is also measures the subject's level of disagreement with statements stressing the equality of different religions and the worthiness of religious Others. Unsurprisingly, high-RWAs who identified as fundamentalist Christians scored high in religious ethnocentrism.

Then Altemeyer went a step further, wondering if those who did score high on the Ethnocentrism scale were open to this truth about themselves. He added a question to the test, asking the subject if they would wish to know their score if it turned out it showed them to be highly prejudiced?

In one such experiment, 76% of the low-RWA subjects said they would want to know their score; only 55% of the high-RWAs wanted to know. Then, for clarification, he reversed the question, in a subsequent experiment: the final question asked if the subject if they would wish to know their score if it awarded them a *low* score? The low-RWA subjects scored about the same – 71%; but this time, 77% of the high-RWAs wanted to know their score. Conclusion: low-RWAs are equally interested in good or bad news about themselves, while high-RWAs are very open to good news but less open to bad.

Altemeyer's curiosity was derived from noting that highly prejudiced people tend to deny being so. This lack of self-awareness, he concluded, was essentially tribal: "If you spend a lot of time around rather prejudiced people," he wrote, "you can easily think your own prejudices are normal."

Why some people love authoritarians

I've written in the past that authoritarianism is not necessarily a good thing or a bad thing in and of itself, but becomes constructive or destructive depending on the social context in which it presents.

I hope I've gotten better at writing about the subject and conveying the key ideas, because we're living in an increasingly-authoritarian world, and that's not a good thing, and it's important to talk about it openly and frequently. To that end, I've discovered a short video of exceptional clarity that explains the subject concisely, yet insightfully. The YouTube link to the video is given below.

I want to summarize its contents, but before I do that, I'll briefly recap the pros and cons of Authoritarianism and its opposite, Egalitarianism.

Authoritarian personalities tend to:

- Desire strong leadership
- Obey authority
- Favor hierarchical social order
- Abhor uncertainty
- Resist change
- Feel unsafe, in a wide range of circumstances
- Believe in zero-sum scenarios
- Be very loyal
- Contribute generously to the well-being of the tribe

For context, let's remember that egalitarian personalities tend to:

- Prefer decision-by-consensus to the leadership of an individual
- Embrace change
- Seek novelty
- Take risks
- Distrust authority
- Be more loyal to ideas than to people

- Be more comfortable with uncertainty
- Favor an equal, distributed social order
- Contribute generously to the well-being of the tribe)

Taken as a whole, it's easy to see that all of these traits potentially have considerable merit in a community; there is room for all of them, and a role for every member, whichever traits they possess.

In Paleolithic societies, individuals with the Authoritarian traits listed above (remember, these are ultimately genetic personality and behavioral factors, not political or ideological distinctions) would have made a good Fire-Tender – a person who could be counted on to safeguard the tribe through the long night by keeping the bonfire going, to discourage attacks by predators.

But we are not living in the Paleolithic Era anymore. And the *mis*-application of Authoritarian tendencies, given our utterly different modern context, can be catastrophic. A modern Authoritarian may tend to:

- Submit to an unworthy leader simply because they make them feel safe;
- Be vulnerable to manipulation by way of falsehoods triggering fear responses;
- Accept misinformation about those in other tribes designed to render them "dangerous" or "enemies";
- Believe in zero-sum scenarios (where there must be a loser for every winner) without justification, creating a false defensiveness;

- Be dismissive of facts, data, reason, logic, and evidence, when they challenge ideas or beliefs that promote an emotional feeling of safety and security;
- Be willing to suspend equality and fairness, and become accepting of unethical behavior in a leader, if feelings of dread or danger are present.

And this describes what we see all around us, of course, most every day today. Authoritarianism is commonplace; its disciples are numerous. And there is no shortage of social dominators waiting to exploit them.

Now, to the video. It can be found here, if you wish to check it out yourself:

https://www.youtube.com/watch?v=qw8yJ92c_Ds

It opens with the citing of a 2017 National Academy of Sciences study, "Dominant Leader vs. Prestige Leader", which found that people living in zip codes with a history of economic hardship were more likely to support authoritarian leaders in their communities.

It then cites another 2017 study from CNBC, "Why Voters Might Be Choosing Authoritarian Leaders", a three-decade inquiry that surveyed people all over the world, finding that people tend to lean toward Authoritarian leaders in times of economic uncertainty – and that in such times, they are more likely to accept the suspending of democratic norms and to be more tolerant of unethical behavior in their leaders.

It notes a study on Pacific Standard, "The Terrifying Trait That Trump Triggers", which quantifies Authoritarians of making up roughly one-third of the populations of 29 different democracies around the world, but that in such countries, the tendencies of these Authoritarians tend to remain dormant until triggered by some threat (real or perceived). This brings us to the conclusion that it is not that economic uncertainty or other social threats cause people to become Authoritarian, but that 1/3 of the population already possesses Authoritarian tendencies, and threats will cause those tendencies to emerge.

The video explains that the Authoritarian mindset is all-pervasive, not just a batch of situational responses. Authoritarians, for instance, prioritize certain qualities in their children over others – obedience, good manners, and good behavior over independence, curiosity, and critical thinking.

Finally, the video noted that a 2017 *Politico Magazine* study, "Predicting Whether You're a Trump Supporter", reported that an Authoritarian mindset was the sole statistically significant variable predictive of Trump support.

In our current national moment, we see that Authoritarians seem impervious to all inputs from anyone *but* the strongman leaders they follow: no amount of new information, data, facts, logic, or reason can penetrate their thinking. And this should be no surprise; they consider all such inputs to be suspect, efforts to subvert them, dangers to be resisted at all costs. Their emotional investment in the sense of safety and security they derive from their tribe supersedes everything else.

But we need people of *all* cognitive styles and mindsets in the world today, despite the dangers of those misapplied. Everyone has value, and everyone can contribute meaningfully. But an explicitly Authoritarian society under an explicitly Authoritarian strongman leader is the path to ruin: it will result in the loss of liberty, the proliferation of inequality, a landscape of manipulation and persecution. Authoritarianism must be kept in check.

The solution, per the video, is to support and promote those social policies that promote safety and stability, which reduce the triggering of Authoritarian responses – fair taxation, readily-available healthcare, affordable education, sustainable energy, free and fair elections. The presence of such resources promote feelings of safety and security, diminishing the threat posed by social dominators hoping to acquire power.

Rising Authoritarianism today

Authoritarianism is rising in the US today – and around the world. The intense interconnectedness of everything and everyone, enabled by the Internet and the social media it hosts, makes the work of authoritarian leaders easier than it's ever been, and empowers those leaders to spray the disinformation, propaganda, and toxic rhetoric all over their followers like a firehose.

Even experts like Altemeyer are hard-pressed to produce a solution to this problem, though one ray of hope is that the mindset is largely biological; authoritarianism is enabled in individual minds by a propensity for greater fear than most, combined with a lower level of social information processing. Those are genetically-linked brain features, making it probable that there's a limit to the number of authoritarian-leaning minds in any given population. Statistics from around the world suggest that that number is roughly 35 percent.

It should also be clear to even the most casual observer of today's flame wars on social media that there is no talking an authoritarian follower off the ledge. It is useless to argue with them, for all the reasons Altemeyer (and others) have articulated.

What's the Woke response here? A big part of it is the pursuit of cognitive diversity, already covered above; in a nutshell, the biggest step forward is to *break up or dilute social echo chambers everywhere you can.* Authoritarianism is weakened when diversity is strengthened.

Oh, and *vote...*

War

"Either man will abolish war," said the progressive philosopher Bertrand Russell, "or war will abolish man."

In his 2012 book *The End of War*, science writer John Horgan tells of Wesleyan University's David Adams, a psychologist who polled his students in the 1980s, asking them what they thought about war. The results were discouraging. Almost one-third answered "Yes" when asked whether "wars are inevitable because human beings are naturally aggressive" - and an even more discouraging 40 percent said "Yes" to the statement "War is intrinsic to human nature."

Horgan reported that Adams had written, "These results support the need for a worldwide educational campaign to dispel the myth that war is instinctive, intrinsic to human nature, or unavoidable because of an alleged biological bias.

Horgan reported further that Adams and 19 colleagues met in Spain in 1986, in a conference sponsored by the United Nations, to present the following five propositions:

1. It is scientifically incorrect to say that we have inherited a tendency to make war from our

animal ancestors;

2. It is scientifically incorrect to say that war or any other violent behavior is genetically programmed into our human nature;

3. It is scientifically incorrect to say that in the course of human evolution there has been a selection for aggressive behavior more than for other kinds of behavior;

4. It is scientifically incorrect to say that humans have a "violent brain";

5. It is scientifically incorrect to say that war is caused by "instinct" or any single motivation.

The Seville Statement, as it was called, wrapped up by stating "that biology does not condemn humanity to war, and that humanity can be freed from the bondage of biological pessimism... the same species who invented war is capable of inventing peace. The responsibility lies within each of us.

After building the case that war is a choice, that resource scarcity is no excuse, and that the correct view of war is as a cultural contagion, Horgan presents his vision for the end of war, offering a handful of universal rules:

- Indiscriminate killing, of the sort that happens when mines, bombs and drones are used, must be ruled out;
- The highest priority in conflict between nations must be the minimization of civilian casualties (Horgan suggests that the de-escalation policies commonly adopted by police be used as a model);

- Any armed aggression between nations should be architected in such a way as to bring about its own obsolescence (long-term consequences should be the highest consideration).

And finally, Horgan underscores his thesis with a recap of the "Prehistory of Violence," much of which we've already reviewed. His recaps include the following:

- 20,000 years ago: oldest skeleton bearing uncontested indications (an arrowhead in the body, among other things) of homicide, discovered in the Nile Valley;
- 13,000 years ago: the oldest mass grace, Cemetery 117;
- 10,000 years ago: "irrefutable evidence" of organized warfare discovered in northern Mesopotamia, including spears and arrow points, fortifications, and bones with signs of violence.

The point: the appearance of organized warfare in human prehistory was both abrupt and recent. There are no mass graves dating back into the Paleolithic, no patterns of bone damage, no stockpiles of weapons. There is plenty of evidence of human cooperation – and none of systemic aggression.

War is a recent innovation. And John Horgan, Douglas Fry, and Raymond Kelly, among others, believe it can be banished forever.

But what about peace? What is its true history in the human adventure, and how do we bring it forth permanently?

Douglas Fry, in his book *The Human Potential for Peace*, quotes Charles Darwin in *The Descent of Man*:

> "No tribe could hold together if murder, robbery, treachery, etc., were common; consequently such crimes within the limits of the same tribe 'are branded with everlasting infamy;'"

He also quotes anthropologist Brian Ferguson:

> "The image of humanity, warped by bloodlust, inevitably marching off to kill, is a powerful myth and an important prop of militarism in our society. Despite its lack of scientific credibility, there will
> remain those 'Hard-headed realists' who continue to believe in it, congratulating themselves for their
>
> 'courage to face the truth,' resolutely oblivious to the myth behind their 'reality'."

And back to Darwin:

> "As man advances in civilization, and small tribes are united into larger communities, the simplest reason would tell each individual that he ought to extend his social instincts

and sympathies to all the other members of
the same nation, though personally unknown
to him. This point being once reached, there is
only an artificial barrier to prevent his
sympathies extending to the men of all
nations and races."

Fry invests considerable effort in articulating case studies of peaceful behaviors among aboriginal groups, detailing their conflict management practices, and demonstrating the utility and portability of those practices. He also examines a broad range of social organization paradigms, weighing the quality of each in maintaining peace.

Frans de Waal provides a biological foundation for a key component of peaceful coexistence – reconciliation behaviors – in Thomas Gregor's *A Natural History of Peace*.

He begins by providing three evolutionary mechanisms by which aggression is controlled in primate groups: Risk of Injury/Energy Expenditure; Memory of Prior Defeats/Injuries; and Value of Cooperation/Threat to Group Membership.

He then frames his argument by evaluating two competing hypotheses regarding the effects of aggression on social relations. The first is a *dispersal hypothesis*, which predicts that losers would socially avoid winners, the second is a *reconciliation hypothesis*, which predicts that individuals will attempt to repair relationships to restore social value. He and his team then tested the two hypotheses through observation of a range of different primates, capturing patterns of reconciliation.

His finding was that both patterns are frequently displayed: dispersal is commonplace following aggressive confrontation, but reconciliation will follow after a brief period of time.

Anthropologist Leslie Sponsel, also writing in *A Natural History of Peace*, makes the case that social mechanisms for implementing peace as a global default already exist, summarizing:

> "Humans have evolved both biological and cultural behavioral mechanisms to promote nonviolence and peace as well as to avoid, reduce, and resolve conflict and violence. Indeed ethnography does provide *heuristic precedents and models* of sociocultural systems that are relatively nonviolent and peaceful."

Economist Kenneth Boulding, in the same volume, builds a case for global peace as an inevitable emergent feature of *adaptive learning*, as the nations of the world face an increasing stream of unique challenges. He also offers the optimistic reminder that peace is now a formal research topic:

> "...we are looking for a dialectics of learning rather than a dialectics of struggle. One of the hopeful signs emerging from this search has been the development of the peace-research movement of the last 30 or 40 years, which

essentially defines peace as creative
conflict and a learning process as over against
the old dialectic that cannot live without an
enemy."

Torture

Beyond any dispute of its relative ineffectiveness, however, the Woke take is simple: torture is barbaric. Monstrous. Indefensible.

It is illegal in the US, and was banned by a consortium of nations in 1948 in the Universal Declaration of Human Rights (referred to above in "Rights and Freedoms") issued by the United Nations. It is condemned by the Geneva Conventions, the International Covenant on Civil and Political Rights, and the UN's Convention against Torture and Other Cruel, Inhuman or Degrading Treatment or Punishment.

Then again, the Military Commissions Act of 2006, under which the Bush Administration adopted an array of questionable practices in the shadow of the war in Iraq, pulled the US away from its commitment to eschew torture, and drew the rebuke of the United Nations – which the Bush Administration dismissed. Military officials went so far as to dissemble over the issue, insisting in public briefings and written statements that techniques such as waterboarding, which it had aggressively employed, did not constitute torture – leading a judge in the UK to note that "America's idea of what is torture... does not appear to coincide with that of most civilized nations."

Amnesty International rebuked the Act for its destruction of mechanisms for judicial review in the holding of enemy combatants for trial (suspension of *habeas corpus*), as well as its removal of provision for the prosecution of interrogators and soldiers supporting them (a reversal of the War Crimes Act).

The Human Rights Measurement Initiative consequently awarded the US a score of 3.6/10 for its upholding of "the right to freedom free from torture and ill-treatment."

Then there's Guantánamo Bay, in Cuba, where the US installed a "black site" at the naval base there (along with additional black sites in Iraq and Afghanistan), where torture became routine following the 9/11 attacks, as part of Bush's "War on Terror".

Put simply, the US legacy of torture is one of shame and stain.

That the civilized world regards the use of torture with horror, and considers America's indulgence a failure of moral leadership, is clear. What should be added is that these condemnations go beyond criticism of the practice and recognition of its barbarism; they are a recognition that the torturer, at the individual and national levels, is acting not only to achieve a military or punitive result – they are parading power for its own sake, in the service of fear and intimidation.

This enrages the Woke as much or more than the barbarism of the act itself, and rightly so; torture, for millennia, has been not just horrific for the terrors it induces in the moment, but for its effectiveness in breaking those who endure it, often permanently. Torture is a haunting of the tortured by the torturer, the ultimate dominance. To a Woke mind, it's hard to imagine anything more offensive.

PTSD / Veterans

Post-Traumatic Stress Disorder – PTSD – is a label covering a broad range of symptoms, severity levels, and durations. It can last a brief time or a lifetime; its effects can be as mild as insomnia or as severe as complete physical collapse. Common symptoms include nightmares, flashbacks, difficulty concentrating or sleeping, paranoia, irritability, agitation, feelings of guilt, alcoholism or substance abuse, and self-destructive behavior.

This symptoms occur in the wake of some life-threatening event: a car accident, combat, physical attack, sexual assault, even a natural disaster – something that triggers mortal dread.

The mental and emotional disruptions brought on by trauma can be, and usually are, devastating to those who experience them – and they are long-lasting.

Around 6 out of every 100 people in the US has PTSD at some time in their lives, and most people who endure a traumatic event don't end up developing it (according to the National Center for PTSD, about 60% of men and 50% of women experience at least one traumatic event with PTSD-inducing potential at least once in their lives) Many of the people who do experience it recover completely – some with treatment, some without.

And some are more likely to experience it because they have been in military service.

PTSD brought on by war

This, too, is a story all too familiar. While PTSD occurs in people from all kinds of backgrounds, in all kinds of circumstances, it is particularly common in veterans.

The increase, however, isn't what you might guess; while 6 out of 100 average people experience it, in veterans the number only rises to 8. Among these, unsurprisingly, veterans who deploy are more likely to experience it than those who do not.

Current PTSD rates among Vietnam veterans, for instance, rise to 15% for men and 9% for women, according to a 1983 Congressional study. Twice that percentage of men and three times that percentage of women, the study went on to say, experienced PTSD at some point in their lives after Vietnam.

The war on those who went to war

This is one of the biggest reasons why Woke individuals find it so galling when those on the right disparage Americans who have served. In recent years, as authoritarianism has risen in the US, voices on the right have been increasingly hostile and dismissive toward veterans, and lawmakers on the right have seemingly abandoned them.

In 2022, for instance, the Promise to Address Comprehensive Toxics (PACT) Act was poised to finally bring relief to millions of veterans who had been exposed, during service, to toxins with long-term debilitating effects on their health – from Agent Orange in Vietnam to burn pits in Iraq and Afghanistan. Many veterans and their families gathered in Washington, DC on the day of the Senate vote for the Act, only to have 25 Republican senators block it. It represented the largest expansion of care in VA history.

And the leader of the Republican Party at the time – Donald Trump - has, of course, worked tirelessly for years to spread anti-veteran sentiment, calling fallen troops "losers" and former POWs "suckers", per former White House Chief of Staff John Kelly and reporting in *The Atlantic*. Kelly has also stated that his former boss would not be photographed in public with military amputees, saying, "It doesn't look good for me."

Beyond mere disparagement, Trump's assault on veterans included his attempt to gut Medicaid, trimming $1.5 trillion over 10 years: 2 million veterans depend on it.

In the Woke world, war is an atrocity. Walter Cronkite was speaking for us when he said, "War itself is, of course, a form of madness. It's hardly a civilized pursuit. It's amazing how we spend so much time inventing devices to kill each other and so little time working on how to achieve peace."

And beyond PTSD in veterans, the numbers tell us that most of us will know someone suffering from it among our friends, colleagues, or family members at some point in our lives.

When someone we know has it, they should be encouraged to talk to someone about it. And, to be Woke about it, we are equally obliged to speak out against those who disparage who placed themselves in trauma's path to serve their country.

Environmentalism

Defense of the environment through opposition to policies harming it is a cornerstone of Woke culture, and a common anti-Woke point of attack.

There is much to say about both of these specific environmental issues – driving other species to extinction and damaging the atmosphere. But these subjects are already well-covered elsewhere; the more enlightening discussion concerns the Woke/anti-Woke conflict itself, where the environment is concerned.

Why is this the case? Because those who attack people defending the environment have begun doing so even when the attacked are on their side of the ideological fence.

On the surface, GOP efforts to smear Woke environmental concerns might be framed as purely political.

For instance, in elections held in the fall of 2023, GOP candidates made attacks on environmental initiatives centerpieces of their campaigning, according to a report in *ClimateWire*: In New Jersey, they attacked offshore wind; in Virginia, it was the state's electric vehicle mandates. And in coal-producing Kentucky, they went after the Democratic governor for bringing attracting two battery plants to the state.

The working theory behind this is that the GOP's new obsession with this particular corner of Woke is to distract the world from the overturning of *Roe v. Wade*, which is crippling them at the polls. (It didn't work, by the way; Democrats did historically well at the ballot box that year.) But something more is at work. More on that momentarily.

There are still GOP voices out there who actually persist in the belief that climate change is a hoax; presidential candidate Vivek Ramaswamy, for instance, has said, "The reality is, more people are dying of bad climate change policy than they are of actual climate change." What exactly that is supposed to mean is not altogether clear, but he went on to join the *drill, baby, drill* bandwagon the GOP has been on for the better part of two decades now, and which Trump has declared he will proceed with if re-elected. (It's encouraging that when Ramaswamy uttered the word *hoax*, he was booed by the audience.)

Nikki Haley, also a contender for the GOP presidential nomination, said, "Is climate change real? Yes, it is; but if you want to go and really change the environment, then we need to start telling China and India that they have to lower their emissions."

Responding to comments by Ramaswamy and other GOP candidates, Climate Power wrote that "2024 will be a climate election – and Republicans will face real consequences for their ongoing denials."

The gravity of GOP solidarity on opposing climate action is not lost on Woke experts, of course. Climatologist Michael Mann, for instance, has declared that the GOP "is not just a threat to the nation; it's a threat to the planet."

Christopher Barnard, president of the American Conservation Coalition, tweeted "Young Americans – including 88% of conservatives – want a real plan to tackle climate change."

The piece that doesn't fit

Pushing back against electric cars is one thing; but the GOP has now made it its business to push back against *any* climate-friendly initiative.

In South Carolina, a company called Nucor, which makes steel, has been working out ways to do it that reduce the carbon footprint of the process. That's prudent, because steel manufacturing generates a staggering amount of CO_2. And even if the effort is driven in part by noble intent, the fact is it's just good business: their customers, which include automakers, have made it clear to them that they *want* greener product.

Even so, the ostensibly pro-business GOP politicians of South Carolina have stated that investors who support initiatives like Nucor's are promoting Woke politics and policy, when the focus should be making money. The state's Republican lawmakers have considered a bill that would prohibit state retirement fund managers from factoring in environmental issues when making investment decisions. According to NPR, the state treasurer, Curtis Loftis, said in 2022 that he was pulling $200 million from the investment firm BlackRock because of its consideration of environmental concerns.

And none of that fits. Pro-business GOP officials and politicians attacking business (isn't government supposed to stay out of business's way?), and essentially making its own business decisions based on environmental stance?

ESG

The recent turn toward responsible behavior made by many businesses is often referred to as *ESG* – environmental, social, and (corporate) governance. GOP politicians consider that a "liberal" agenda, and push the idea that companies factoring ESG into their decision-making processes and business policies are abusing their investors' money in the service of progressive politics. For the businesses, ESG makes good business sense: it's about 1) sustainability, and 2) listening to their customers, an overwhelming majority of whom understand that climate change is real, that the environment is in crisis, and that something needs to be done about it.

And the inconvenient fact is that the environment used to actually be a GOP priority: Teddy Roosevelt created the national park system, to create untouchable zones of healthy wilderness in the nations; Richard Nixon created the Environmental Protection Agency.

Now the GOP is trying to employ the power of the state to promote environmentally unfriendly policies even when the private sector prefers the alternative. That is unprecedented, and in direct contrast to its stated long-time values. Trump's administration attempted to force electric companies to stick with coal, *even when other power sources were cheaper.* And other state treasurers are doing as Loftis has done, trying to punish banks for taking responsible climate action.

What is this really about? It's clearly not about supporting the free market and opposing government interference. Are GOP politicians simply in the pockets of Big Oil? Some of them, certainly, but not all of them, and the political appointees putting muscle into the GOP's attempts to punish ESG-friendly companies don't need campaign financing.

Paul Krugman of the *New York Times* has pointed out that the Biden Administration's Inflation Reduction Act, arguably the greenest bill in history, has opened up floodgates of business opportunity, and received the endorsement of BP, Shell, and other Big Oil entities. The GOP doesn't care.

So what does Krugman think is going on here?

"What has happened, I'd argue, is that environmental policy has been caught up in the culture war - which is, in turn, largely driven by issues of race and ethnicity," he wrote. "This, I suspect, is why the partisan divide on the environment widened so much after America elected its first Black president.

"One especially notable aspect of *The Times*'s investigative report on state treasurers' punishing corporations seeking to limit greenhouse gas emissions is the way these officials condemn such corporations as 'woke.'

"Wokeness normally means talking about racial and social justice. On the right - which is increasingly defined by attempts to limit the rights of Americans who aren't straight white Christians - it has become a term of abuse. Teaching students about the role of racism in American history is bad because it's woke. But so, apparently, are many other things, like Cracker Barrel offering meatless sausage and being concerned about climate change.

"This may not make much sense intellectually, but you can see how it works emotionally. Who tends to worry about the environment? Often, people who also worry about social justice - either that, or global elites. (Climate science is very much a global enterprise.)

"Even Republicans who have to know better won't break with the party's anti-science position. As governor of Massachusetts, Mitt Romney had a decent environmental record; yet he joined every other Republican member of Congress in voting against the I.R.A.

"What this means is that those people hoping for bipartisan efforts on climate are probably deluding themselves. Environmental protection is now part of the culture war, and neither policy details nor rational argument matters."

Is Krugman right? It's pretty hard to refute his argument; the GOP's attitude toward climate activism and pro-green policy doesn't make sense, viewed through the lens of its own purported value system, and some of their antagonist members are coming right out and saying it – this is about their War on Woke, nothing more.

Medical Ethics

As medical science has progressed, there have been all too many who have crossed the ethical line of doing harm to human beings in the pursuit of knowledge.

And a line it is: on one side is the imperative to discover, the legitimate need to push back the veil of ignorance wherever and whenever we can, to add to the human trove of understanding that can, one day, take us to the stars. That's a vital imperative; an essential imperative. It's one we dare not abandon, lest ignorance reclaim us and lead us to extinction.

Yet, on the other side of that line, we have the even greater imperative to respect life for the incalculably treasure it is, preserving it and nurturing it at all costs.

That's not an easy line to honor, when human weakness intrudes: greed; impatience; nationalism; vanity – the list of flaws in humanity that can push us across that line is long.

Here are some examples:

- In the infamous "Tuskegee Study of Untreated Syphilis in the Negro Male", performed by the US Public Health Service, almost 400 black men who had syphilis were offered treatment but were not told that they had syphilis, and the treatment they were given wasn't for syphilis; they were simply studied to chart the progression of the disease. When penicillin became available, the infected men were blocked from receiving it, so as not to interfere with the study. By its end, only 74 were still alive; 28 had died of syphilis, more than 100 died of related complications; 40 of their wives had become infected, and 19 of their children were born with congenital syphilis. Only when the study was made public, sparking outrage, was the study finally shut down.

- In 1874, Dr. Roberts Bartholow diagnosed a lesion on the head of an Irish servant woman, Mary Rafferty, as terminal – but didn't tell her so, as he saw in her a research opportunity. He inserted electrodes into her exposed brain matter in order to measure her responses. The process put her in a coma, from which she recovered in three days – but she died the following day of a massive seizure.

- In 1986, the US House Committee on Energy and Commerce published a report on federal experimentation on thousands of US citizens over decades, titled "American Nuclear Guinea Pigs: Three Decades of Radiation Experiments on US Citizens". The report described studies wherein mentally ill children and conscientious objectors had been fed radioactive food; radium rods had been inserted into the noses of children; releasing radioactive material over US and Canadian cities, in order to measure the effects of fallout; and injecting pregnant women and babies with radioactive materials to measure the genetic effects.

- Sonoma State Hospital in California took in mentally disabled children between 1955 and 1960, performing painful experiments on them without any consent, including spinal taps. It was later learned that the brain of every child who had died of cerebral palsy was removed and studied – again, without any consent.

- For an astonishing 38 years, Dr. Leo Stanley, a surgeon at San Quentin Prison, performed hundreds of experiments on prisoners – implanting the testicles of executed prisoners into living ones; implanting the testicles of goats, rams, and other animals into prisoners; and performing eugenics experiments and sterilizations on prisoners in an effort to perfect techniques for rejuvenation and regulate criminal impulses.

- The US military's Project Bluebird included the dosing of over 7,000 US military personnel with LSD, without their knowledge or consent, as part of a study intended to evaluate drugs that could be used effectively in interrogation. More than 1,000 of these unwilling subjects experienced depression and epilepsy, and many attempted suicide.

- Toying with the notion of using mustard gas

on Axis enemies if they themselves resorted to
biological warfare, the US military used it on
1,200 soldiers in Panama without telling them
what it was in 1942. They suffered horrifying
burns, for which they were promptly treated,
and were threatened with military prison if
they ever revealed what had been done to
them.

Finally, there's the granddaddy of all unethical
research programs – the CIA's MKULTRA initiative,
started in 1953, to study mind control techniques. It
soaked up $25 million, funded hundreds of experiments
on countless human subjects (the exact number is
unknown). CIA director Richard Helms once wrote a
memo that included:

> "We intend to investigate the development of a
> chemical material which causes a reversible,
> nontoxic aberrant mental state, the specific
> nature of which can be reasonably well predicted
> for each individual. This material could
> potentially aid in discrediting individuals,
> eliciting information, and implanting suggestions
> and other forms of mental control."

Helms himself shut down MKULTRA in 1973 to
avoid its public exposure, ordering all records
destroyed.

What is most horrifying about these events, a staggering number of which were undertaken by the US government and military, is how perfectly they mirror the scientific research methods of the Nazi regime. The justification, of course, was always, "the ends justifies the means." Innocent and ignorant subjects were sacrificed on the altar of science by unethical or unscrupulous manipulators, to advance some cause thought to be more important than human dignity.

It's an ethical conundrum, but not much of one. At one point *does* the end justify the means? When do we say that it's worth a handful of lives to do this research, if it ultimately saves millions of lives? Who makes that call? Under what restrictions would we permit that research to move forward?

Until we answer those questions – and, clearly, they need to be answered – we need to back away, and put human rights and dignity first.

Capitalism vs. Socialism

It's an age-old debate: are capitalism and socialism mutually exclusive? Is one good, the other evil? Strong opinions abound. We even fight this battle in our popular entertainment.

Star Wars, Star Trek, and Macroeconomic Theory

Silicon Valley venture capitalist Peter Thiel, in a conversation with *New York Times* columnist Maureen Dowd, weighed in on that most famous of geek controversies: *Star Wars or Star Trek?*

Though rich, powerful and at least nominally conservative, Thiel is most qualified to join this particular fray. Though he hasn't been spotted at many West Coast Comic-Cons, he nonetheless can claim geek cred by way of his investment choices: he pals around with Elon Musk and Mark Zuckerberg. Thiel himself might not pass for geek, but he loves to fund it.

The interview drew the attention of Manu Saadia, author of *Trekonomics: The Economics of Star Trek.*

Writing for *The New Yorker*, Saadia took note of Thiel's fanboy preference – *Star Wars* – and took note of his reason why.

"Capitalism," he answered.

"The whole plot of *Star Wars* starts with Han Solo having this debt that he owes, and so the plot in *Star Wars* is driven by money.

"*Star Trek*," on the other hand, "is the communist one."

Put simply, *Star Wars* appeals to Thiel's more libertarian sensibilities, while *Star Trek* evokes the horrors of a capitalism-free universe with lots of equality, no poverty, and completely egalitarian opportunity. In an essay published by the Cato Institute, he wrote that technology is often a dangerous distraction to social attention; freedom, he wrote, is a product of political thought, not technological advancement. And *Star Trek* seems to say the opposite.

Star Wars "is in fact much closer to home that *Star Trek*," Saadia wrote in *The New Yorker*. "Forget the lightsabers and the Force: the essential story of the films is familiar, a techified version of a Wild West that existed only in Buffalo Bill's travelling revue and its celluloid successors, the Westerns. In *Star Wars*, criminal potentates hire bounty hunters to recover debts from roguish smugglers. Robots are menial servants and sycophants rather than colleagues, and human slavery persists. Unelected tyrants and religious zealots make policy by fiat. A blaster, or a Death Star, is the only real guarantor of life and liberty. Fate and the lottery of birth reign supreme. It is a libertarian's fever dream, a distilled expression of the idea that the greater good is best served through unfettered (and, if necessary, brutal) economic competition.

"This, rather than the liberal-democratic setting of the *USS Enterprise*, is the political environment in which Thiel seems to feel most comfortable... in [his Cato Institute essay] he places 'confiscatory taxes, totalitarian collectives, and the ideology of the inevitability of the death of every individual' in opposition to 'authentic human freedom.' Only the strong and lucky, like Han Solo, should survive."

On the other hand, in the *Star Trek* universe, "technological progress is inseparable from society and politics," Saadia wrote. "As even quasi-fans will recall, the TV shows and films feature a machine called the replicator, which can produce any inanimate matter on demand – food, drink, warp-drive parts... The replicator solves, albeit fictionally, what John Maynard Keynes once called 'the economic question' – that is, the imbalance between supply and demand, and the resulting need for markets and price mechanisms to allocate scarce resources. The society of *Star Trek* has decided not to exact a fee for the use of the machine. Thus the replicator can be an engine both for the equal distribution of wealth and for personal enrichment. It does not bring about social change on its own. The post-scarcity world in *Star Trek* is the result of a political decision, not of pure technological progress."

It's an interesting new take on a very old debate: *Star Wars* as a 'libertarian fever dream,' *Star Trek* as the ultimate 'liberal-democratic' ideal. Yet it's spot-on accurate as sociopolitical characterization, when we consider the feudal mythologies that inspired George

Lucas and the contemporary philosophy behind Gene Roddenberry's overt progressive manifesto.

In the *Star Wars* universe, life is cheap and freedom precious, because it's in such short supply. Authoritarianism reigns, in constant tension with the rage of the oppressed, with survival-of-the-fittest as the rule – and technology is leveraged only to serve this dynamic, never to rise above it.

In the *Star Trek* universe, life is revered and freedom the default, in bountiful supply. Egalitarianism reigns, and the right of self-determination is the highest rule. Technology is leveraged in its service, overtly bolstering equality, rather than enabling its antithesis.

This leads us to a very interesting question: what, exactly, is the difference in these two universes, this opposing visions of human socioeconomic order?

The *Star Wars*-Wild West analogy might lead us astray here. It seeks to situate Han Solo, Luke Skywalker and company in a resource-sparse economy, where smugglers thrive, moisture farmers eek out a living wringing water from the air, and energy is flat-out hard to come by. Poverty is always within shouting distance, and human beings are used as beasts of labor.

Star Trek, on the other hand, shows us a society built on an energy-rich economy, where no one goes hungry, every living being is respected and nurtured by the society, and boundless accomplishment is possible.

It is easily argued that free and plentiful energy is the key difference between these two socioeconomic models.

But that argument is just as easily dismissed. In the *Star Wars* universe, all weapons – *even swords* – are energy-based; ships that are orders of magnitude more massive than the *USS Enterprise* roam the stars; planets can be blown to pieces. If anything, the *Star Wars* economy is *more* energy-rich than *Star Trek*'s.

We're looking, then, not at technology, nor even at energy supply, to pin down the critical difference in these two economies. And Peter Thiel's attitudes, per Saadia's essay, underscore it:

> "What is anathema to Thiel in *Star Trek* is the notion, drawn from Isaac Asimov's fiction, that the market is but a temporary solution to imbalances in supply and demand, and that technology and plenty will eventually make it obsolete. *Star Trek* replicators are nothing but Asimov's robots disguised as coffee machines, let loose on the world as a public good. They dissolve the need for a pricing mechanism. They represent the logical endpoint of the Industrial Revolution, when all human labor has been offloaded to machines. *Star Trek* and Asimov remind us that the market and all the behaviors associated with it are temporary and historically contingent. If that is so, then what Thiel thinks of human nature and motivations – that people are competitive, acquisitive, greedy – is temporary and contingent, too."

And there we have it.

Star Wars and *Star Trek* are not simply two very different visions of human society. They are two very different – and competing – views of human *nature*.

Are human beings competitive, acquisitive, greedy? That's an easy argument to make.

The follow-up questions are not so easy: have we always been so? And are we necessarily so?

Star Wars says Yes.

Star Trek says No.

Human Nature, Through the Economic Lens

Perhaps the most important point made in the essay above comes at the end of the Saadia quote:

> "*Star Trek* and Asimov remind us that
> the market and all the behaviors
> associated with it are temporary and
> historically contingent. If that is so, then
> what Thiel thinks of human nature and
> motivations – that people are
> competitive, acquisitive, greedy – is
> temporary and contingent, too."

This sums up the capitalism/socialism debate in just two sentences. Those who advocate for capitalism as the ideal human socioeconomic system do so on the basis of the conviction, which they attribute to Adam Smith, that everyone acts (economically) in their own self-interest.

Layered beneath this belief, one will also find in their rhetoric the associated assumptions that human beings are naturally competitive, acquisitive, greedy – assumptions Thiel has frequently confirmed.

To get to the truth of this, then, we would need to challenge those assumptions: are human beings naturally competitive, acquisitive, and greedy?

A common theme in *Trek* is that a civilization is stronger when it is united in common purpose – an idea Kirk promoted in both the moment and, for civilizations he felt like meddling in, the long run.

Whether he was meddling or not, it's certainly true that nothing unites a society like common purpose. All too often, that purpose is war – but that very example underscores the point.

Anyone who has been to war, risked everything in defense of home, family and country, understands the concept of 'Band of Brothers' – a group of young men are thrown together by an imminent threat to their homeland, rapidly trained and shipped out to some front line where a formidable enemy waits, where bullets are flying and bombs exploding.

And those young men bond rapidly and deeply, to the point that the survivors will be reuniting a half-century later, to celebrate their bond and renew their mutual gratitude.

This experience is rare. Few things bring people together like the response to existential threat. In two world wars, we saw this response, this transformation that forever altered men in the battlefield, women supporting them in a wide range of roles, and the society they returned to serve.

Fighting to survive, side by side – it is hard to imagine a more powerful social force.

In the modern era, it is the rare exception: few of us fight for our lives, ever, let alone for extended periods, side by side with others. Our lives are very easy and trouble-free, compared to our distant ancestors – for whom the fight to survive, side by side, was never-ending, from birth to death.

A number of threats persisted for the 3+ million years the human line was evolving, but the greatest was predation: located in south-central Africa, we lived among the most vicious, efficient hunters roaming the Earth at that time – the members of the *Panthera* genus. The Big Cats.

We know from the ratio of skeletons recovered in Africa that Paleolithic humans had very limited lifespans. But this wasn't due to genetics – Cro-Magnon humans were genetically identical to us, and we can live more than 100 years. It wasn't due to famine – famine didn't exist; or disease, which existed, but which didn't impact us heavily until we began living in close, largely unsanitary groups.

We seldom lived to 30 because we were likely to be killed and eaten before we reached that age. The predation of leopards, tigers, and other cats was systematic, and it took us many tens of thousands of years to develop defenses. During that phase of our physical and social evolution, our mutual reliance in detecting and fleeing predators, prior to (or upon) attack, necessarily required focused attention, strong communication, and an investment in one another's survival. The invention of the spear didn't diminish this reliance; if anything, it greatly strengthened it, because communication in coordinated counter-attack was necessarily even deeper, and the trust of the tribe in its defenders heightened, as they undertook risks previously unimagined, in defense of the group and their young.

And this wasn't the only mutual reliance: while the hunter-gatherer lifestyle offers a wide range of sustenance and many modes of acquiring food, it nonetheless requires deep mutual reliance and trust to cope with the migration of animals that could provide food, adapting to weather affecting the presence of edible plants, and anticipating cold weather and storms. Internally, cooperative efforts such as the manufacturing of survival-critical artifacts, maintenance of fire, and the preparation and distribution of food all required deep familial cooperation. The members of a human tribe were together 24/7 – sleeping, waking, hunting, mating, child-rearing – surviving. Birth to death, for hundreds of thousands of years.

Human beings are the ultimate cooperators.

It is difficult to imagine a more intimate life. It is hard to fathom deeper common purpose.

And if any further evidence of *Homo sapiens*' strong capacity for cooperation was the key to our eventual survival and dominance, our entry into Paleolithic Europe sets aside all doubt.

The Savanna Principle

Taking delight in the differences between human beings necessarily begins with enjoying them in the first place.

How this state is achieved and how it works, once achieved, are questions central to our understanding of human nature, and have been for thousands of years. Are human beings naturally competitive or cooperative? Are we instinctively wary of others, or inwardly welcoming? Are the answers to these questions the same today as they were 100,000 years ago, and if not, why not?

That human beings are the ultimate cooperators in the annals of life is beyond dispute: no other species comes close to having achieved what we achieve when we operate collectively, for good or ill. But what drives that cooperation? Economics? Improving our survival by controlling the environment? Tribal dynamics?

Satoshi Kanazawa,[1] an evolutionary psychologist at the London School of Economics, had a different idea. In 2004, he proposed the Savanna Principle, which suggests that human beings remain adapted to the environment in which we evolved – central Africa – and that many of

---

[1] It should be noted that Kanazawa is a controversial figure in evolutionary psychology – not for his Savanna Principle, but for the contentious suggestion in other published work that disease and poverty are rampant in Africa because of lower native IQ, and the even more contentious suggestion that black women are objectively less attractive than other women. In response to these, his university forbade him from publishing in non-peer-reviewed sources for a period of one year, and 38 of his colleagues censured him in *American Psychology*.

our modern-world dysfunction may be attributed to our inherent incompatibility with the environment we have created for ourselves. Our ancient hunger for sugars, for instance – a survival advantage in an environment protein-rich and sugar-poor, where quick-hit energy and immediate storage of ingested carbohydrates could be a huge benefit – is extremely detrimental to our health in the modern era, where all foods are plentiful and none of us are ever tasked with fleeing from large, fast predators.

We are already neck-deep in that general idea, but Kanazawa adds a wrinkle that we can add to our thinking. The wrinkle we now add is the dopamine *ding*, that rewarding little boost we feel in our brains when we solve a problem, eat a tasty meal, or have sex. Dopamine is our inner assurance that all is right with the world – and we can tie it to a further thought of Kanazawa's.

That idea posits that human tribes on the savanna faced an almost endless series of challenges, puzzles and problems beyond the ken of any individual – and that a human tribe could, collectively, thrive in such a world far better than an individual. This idea, which he crafted with Norman Li of Singapore Management University, was dubbed the Savanna Theory of Happiness – that the impulse modern humans feel to be around other humans is a holdover from our savanna days, when there was pleasure in facing the dangers of the world surrounded by other problem-solvers.

(A corollary to this idea is its explanatory force regarding high-IQ individuals, who prefer solitude to a far greater degree – because, the theory suggests, they are superb problem solvers on their own, with less need for the emotional relief of a surrounding tribe.)

When we fold the dopamine *ding* into that theory, we take a huge leap forward: we have a physical, genetically-linked attribute of human cognition (dopamine receptivity) that supports the idea of group selection, that cooperative human groups are subject to an evolutionary driver above the level of personal survival and gene transmission.

Last Humans Standing:
Interspecies Cooperation

It wasn't just cooperation among ourselves that led humankind to survival and success - all primate species cooperate, living and thriving in social groups. *Homo sapiens*, however, took it to the next level: inter-species cooperation.

In 2009, Mietje Germonpre of the Royal Belgian Institute of Natural Sciences established a cranial distinction between canine species - a way of separating dogs from wolves. This development overturned previous estimates of the advent of the domestication of canines in human history (around 18,000 years ago), given the presence of much older skulls in Europe (32,000+ years).

This was a stunning finding. It basically established that when our species invaded and took Europe from the Neanderthals, we did so with canine assistance.

As strategic partnerships go, it couldn't have been a more perfect fit. Humans have an incredibly poor sense of smell, one of the worst in the animal kingdom; dogs, of course, rank near the top, giving Team Sapiens an overwhelming advantage in the hunt. Add to that their auditory range, which extends beyond that of humans, adding significantly to their value as trackers.

Moreover, dogs are possessed of almost human-like loyalty, strengthening the alliance beyond any other domestic bond between human and animal, before or since. Neanderthals couldn't possibly compete – and the question of how Cro-Magnon took over is answered: the human-canine partnership combined the traits of the world's most sensitive trackers with those of the world's most cooperative predators.

It was a piece that had been missing for some time. The fossil and climate records have already informed us of Neanderthal history: they were in Europe more than half a million years in advance of *Homo sapiens*. They had stronger, sturdier physiques; slightly larger brains; sophisticated group behaviors, even comparable culture. Cro-Magnon (modern) humans show up, and the Neanderthals are gone in an eye-blink (possibly as quickly as 2,000 years).

To some degree, we now know, we absorbed them: each of us carries at least a residual smudge of their DNA. But the fact is, we took their territory, and took it quickly. Per anthropologist Pat Shipman, it was human partnership with dogs that made the difference.

With his best friend at his side, the Cro-Magnon out-hunted the neighbors by a wide margin. Humans and dogs together were far more effective that humans alone - and remain so, as hunters, even today.

The Prehistory of Altruism

The German physicist Stefan Klein offers a bold new insight to our consideration of cooperation, and it's this: the purest form of cooperation is contributing with no thought of return – altruism. And in his view, it is altruism that ultimately defines us as human.

Reciprocity is doing something for someone, expecting them to do something in return; cooperation is working together in pursuit of a shared goal, expecting to benefit equally from the outcome. But altruism abandons these expectations; it is action taken on behalf of another person or the group for the sake of the action itself.

No other creature behaves in such a way.

Klein continues, building the case that altruism is innate – built into human genes, alongside cooperation and empathy. His case is simple: it is empirically demonstrable that acts of altruism evoke the same neurological satisfactions in human beings as sex or eating a tasty meal. When we perform an act of kindness or service to another person with no thought or expectation of reward, we feel a sense of pleasure and satisfaction – a *dopamine response*. No one teaches us this feeling; small children experience it when they share a cookie or a toy with a peer (in studies conducted to measure this, facial expressions and vocalizations were used as satisfaction measures).

We experience this pleasure even when the act is remote – when we don't see the response of the person to whom the kindness or service is offered. Anonymous altruism is, in fact, as pleasurable as an in-person act.

Empathy plays a role here. When we perform an altruistic act for another, we are acting in the confidence that their emotional response will be akin to what ours would be, were we on the receiving end of such an act.

And empathy, Klein points out, is a component of trust.

Acts of altruism, then, are signposts of empathetic bonding – and a trust-building mechanism. As such, altruism is elevated to a key influence in human social success.

The Origin of Trust

In *The Moral Molecule: The New Science of What Makes Us Good and Evil*, Paul Zaks painstakingly explains how empathy arises in human beings, becoming trust, enabling our moral selves and social organization – by way of oxytocin.

Oxytocin is central to our neurological machinery, a key player in our emotional selves. It is a peptide hormone, playing roles in sex, birth, breastfeeding, and social bonding. It is the big moving part in the chain of experiences that makes us the most socially successful creatures on earth.

Oxytocin is the source of the contractions women experience in childbirth, a response to the stretching of the cervix; it subsequently enables lactation, triggering the letdown of milk, and its production is perpetuated by the stimulation of the nipples by a suckling infant.

That seems simple enough, but Zaks elaborates in great detail. This birth/breastfeeding mechanism is only the beginning, however. A key point is that oxytocin isn't a female hormone; it is present in both genders, and has many functions beyond breastfeeding.

When an infant feels the skin of her mother's breast against her cheek, she will instinctively turn to the nipple. This 'latch' reflex facilitates mother-child bonding; the mother experiences warm, affectionate feelings for her child as a direct response to the flood of oxytocin.

The thing is... neither the release of oxytocin nor the feelings it inspires are limited to breasts and baby cheeks.

Gentle skin-to-skin contact *in general* inspires the release of oxytocin and its bounty of positive feelings. When we touch someone's face, embrace them, shake their hand, place an arm around them, we trigger a surge of oxytocin in them and in ourselves.

This, Zaks explains, is where empathy ultimately arises. It signals to those we are close to that we are a source of warmth and comfort – and this leads to trust, which in turn leads to social cohesion within groups. Oxytocin intensifies in-group bonding.

That sounds like a pretty big leap. But it's been empirically tested.

One study[2] demonstrated that participants who received nasal infusions of oxytocin had stronger emotional responses to pictures of pained faces of in-group members than they did to pained expressions in out-group members. Further, oxytocin stimulates a desire to protect vulnerable in-group members in

---

[2] "Oxytocin modulates the racial bias in neural responses to others' suffering", F. Sheng et al. *Biological Psychology* 92(2), 380-6.

conflicts between groups: participants in another study[3] who received nasal oxytocin infusions presented more defensive behaviors toward in-group members than out-group members. Many variations on this theme have emerged in research: affection for one's nation, for instance, measured by feelings inspired when seeing the national flag, measurably increases when oxytocin is boosted.

And the neurological machinery that makes this deep bonding happen has been with us for hundreds of thousands of years; civilization has nothing to do with it.

Zaks leaves us with a very broad statement about the crucial role of oxytocin:

> "The 'thou shalt' religious devotion that my mother tried to pound into me faded away a long time ago, but ironically, something at the core has remained. Oxytocin – a reproductive hormone – makes us moral, so ultimately, you could say that we are moral because of our origins as sexual creatures. Which harks back to that very Christian-sounding idea that God is love, or maybe that love is God. But as we saw, *eros* – sex – is only one kind of love, and oxytocin covers all the bases. Oxytocin makes us feel the love for others that's known as *philia*, the familial love known as *storge*, as well as *agape* – transcendence, which can be released during dance, meditation, and

---

[3] "Oxytocin motivates non-cooperation in intergroup conflict to protect vulnerable in-group members", C.K. De Drew et al, *PLOS ONE* 7(11).

magic."

To me, God references notwithstanding, that's pretty *Trek*-sounding.

The Evolution of Cooperation

In his book *Why We Cooperate*, developmental psychologist Michael Tomasello addresses the following question: is cooperation between human beings a naturally emergent behavior or a learned one?

Either way, it's great that it exists, but the implications for our thesis – that human beings possess the inherent goodness in which Gene Roddenberry believed – are profound: if the former, then we have within us what we need to achieve a fully progressive future; if the latter, then it will be a far greater struggle, getting where we want to be.Tomasello begins by pointing to research[4] demonstrating that infants as young as 18 months overwhelmingly attempt to assist adults whose hands are full. He cites this as one of five reasons to believe that this cooperative impulse in very small children is a naturally emergent human trait. It's the first of five:

1. Very small children impulsively help others
    without prompting or training;
2. Parental reward does not alter the outcome of
    #1; the child will impulsively help with or

---

4 *Not by Genes Alone: How Culture Transformed Human Evolution*, Peter Richardson and Robert Boyd. University of Chicago Press, 2006.

without reward;

3. Chimpanzee infants exhibit the same behaviors;
4. Human children exhibit the behavior across a diverse range of cultures;
5. Experiments have shown that helping behavior in young children is mediated by empathy – they will tend to help an adult they perceive to be a victim before helping another.

Tomasello continues to methodically develop a portrait of cooperation as evolutionary, building toward this conclusion: "...the changes we see in human societies beginning with the advent of agriculture and cities are not due, on anyone's account, to any kind of biological adaptation," he wrote. "The changes would seem to be sociological only, given their recency and the fact that by this time modern humans were already spread out all over the glove (so that a species-wide biological change was highly unlikely). What this means is that most, if not all, of the highly complex forms of cooperation in modern industrial societies – from the United Nations to credit card purchases over the Internet – are built primarily on cooperative skills ant motivations biologically evolved for small-group interactions: the kinds of altruistic and collaborative activities that we have seen here in our simple studies of great apes and young children."

We have good reason to believe, then, that the deep cooperation that binds humanity doesn't need to be contrived; it just needs to be awakened.

Homelessness

How serious is the problem of homelessness in the US?

As of the 2020 census, over 500,000 Americans are homeless. About 60 percent of these have access to refuge of some kind in shelters, as the brother of the deceased soldier in the episode did; the available shelters for the homeless in the US can accommodate about 330,000 beds (as of 2022).

The remainder are forced to sleep in the open, unsheltered – on the street, in abandoned buildings, in doorways and parks and other potentially unsafe environments.

About 26 million people in the US have experienced homelessness (as of 2018); more than 75% of these are 25 or older.

The Biden Administration has introduced All In, a federal strategic plan to reduce homelessness in the US by 25% by 2025. The program unites the resources of 19 federal agencies and includes comprehensive input from the people whom it will actually serve – the homeless, 500 of whom testified for the program's presiding council to guide its planning.

The foundations of the program, according to its

website, are equity, data & evidence, and collaboration; its solutions focus on housing & supports, crisis response, and prevention.

The problem of homelessness has its roots in the industrialization of the nation in the 19th century, when cities first began to grow in earnest and urban housing had to keep up. Once the railroads had blanketed the nation, a migrant population of vagrants emerged, and the image of what we now call a "hobo" began to emerge.

The Great Depression added to this population, though federal work programs after World War II had a temporary positive impact. Those gains were undone in the Eighties, when the Reagan Administration's deinstitutionalization of the mentally ill and deep budget cuts to the US Department of Housing and Urban Development sent the number of homeless in the nation soaring again.

A grim scenario was played out in the real world in 1971, when inmates in New York's Attica Correctional Facility revolted to secure better living conditions, resulting in a riot and a four-day standoff in which 33 inmates and 10 correctional officers were killed. That's not quite the same situation as the homeless face today, of course, but it's worth noting that when human beings are treated as something less, the outcome is never good.

Will the current efforts be enough to make a difference? We'll know soon enough; in the meantime, an article ran in the *Los Angeles Times* just as it had finished production, in which then-Mayor Richard Riordan proposed the creation of fenced-in "havens" for the city's homelessness, to make the city's downtown area more desirable for business.

The Right to Die

The common Woke stance is that every individual has the right to choose to live, or not.

People take their own lives all the time, of course, but when we refer to the right to die as such, we are talking about a process involving people other than the person doing the dying: physicians assisting in the suicide, or performing euthanasia when the person dying is unable to execute the act themselves.

There's a lot going on in this issue. There are many reasons why a person might choose to end their own life, and they can't all be covered in a couple of television episodes: terminal illness; physical agony; disaffection; old age. And, as in the episodes, societal deference; unbearable boredom. There is also the issue of choosing not to
live in a vegetative state, wherein an individual can put in place a Do Not Resuscitate order such that wish to have their death proceed if they find themselves in such a state.

Law has been written in the US and around the world, addressing the right to die. Many countries, including Australia, Canada, Germany, the Netherlands, New Zealand, Belgium, and others, have legalized euthanasia.

In some countries, including India and Columbia, it has been made available to the terminally ill. And in some countries, like Peru, it remains illegal.

In the United States, it's more nuanced. There is no blanket law on euthanasia covering all 50 states, but 10 US jurisdictions – California, Colorado, Hawaii, Maine, New Mexico, Oregon, Vermont, Washington, and Washington, DC – have made assisted suicide legal. In Montana, assisted suicide is disputed, though the state's supreme court has ruled that there is no language in precedent or statutes that physician assistance in suicide violates public policy.

Rising support for the Right to Die

Approval of physician-assisted suicide has been increasing over time. Per Pew Research, in 1990, 79% of Americans supported the right to die; by 2005, that number had risen to 84%.

But there's a moral question, too, to do with the circumstances of ending life. In 1990, 55% of Americans believed a person is morally justified in ending their life if they are suffering greatly and will not improve; 49%, in the case of terminal illness; 27%, if they feel life is unbearable; and 29%, if they feel they are an extreme burden to their family. In 2005, those numbers were 60%, 53%, 33%, and 29% respectively.

And over time, the rise in support is more dramatic: in a 1947 Gallop poll, euthanasia only had 37% of the public's approval.

Then there's the role of religion in public opinion on

the issue. Unsurprisingly, those who self-identify as religious and/or attend church regularly are more opposed to euthanasia than those who don't.

The arguments for and against

Arguments in favor of euthanasia include:

- *Primacy of bodily autonomy.* It's my body, I can do as I wish with it
- *Personal agency.* Choosing the time of one's death should be first and foremost the right of the one dying
- *Death with dignity.* It is immoral to insist that a person persist when their personal dignity is compromised

Then again,
- *Religious objections.* People of faith argue that suicide is a mortal sin
- *Support for alternatives.* Some argue that it is immoral to end a life, even a beleaguered one, when other options persist (such as palliative care)
- *Avoiding premature death.* Terminal illnesses don't always turn out to be

Ultimately, the Woke attitude regarding the right to die amounts to the belief that individuals should retain the right to decide for themselves, not just about death, but about *everything* that affects them, so long as their decision does not lead harm to others – that no group, social or religious or political, should be permitted to impose its beliefs and positions on others as public policy unless it is to the good of all.

That means our lives are ours to do with as we wish, and that respect for the choices we make about them is what we should expect of our society.

Religious Indoctrination

It is the position of the Christian Right that the teaching of evolution in public schools opens the minds of children to "blasphemy". We've been hearing it for many decades, starting with the Scopes Monkey Trial in 1925.

Strictly speaking, we've been hearing it a lot longer than that. Religious leaders and the monarchs, oligarchs, and politicians who leverage them have been imposing educational agendas for thousands of years, across continents and cultures. And with the Enlightenment, skirmishes began to erupt, as science and reason began to push back against the authoritarianism of religious authority. The confrontation between the Roman Catholic Church and Galileo springs to mind.

From that day to this, science has been gaining ground and religion has been losing it – leading to Scopes, when a Tennessee schoolteacher stood up against the state's Butler Act, which forbade the teaching of evolution in public schools. John Scopes was unclear on whether he had ever actually mentioned evolution in the classroom, but he deliberately set himself up for prosecution anyway, to bring the debate into public light. He was famously prosecuted by William Jennings

Bryan, and defended by Clarence Darrow. He lost, but was only charged a trifling fine, and his conviction was overturned on a technicality in any case. And the goal of bringing the topic into the national discourse was achieved spectacularly.

Humanism began its rise in the US, with its published manifesto loudly declaring both its fealty to science and empiricism and its independence from religious authority. It proclaimed humankind to be part of nature and that the universe did not have a "creator". Them was fightin' words to Evangelicals, who began to openly mobilize.

In the Sixties, the book *The Genesis Flood* attempted to establish a 6,000-year-old Earth on scientific grounds, giving Young Earth Creationism a big push. The US Supreme Court pushed back, ruling that Epperson v. Arkansas, which established a law against teaching evolution in public schools, violated the Constitution.

In the Seventies, Creations had changed strategies, pushing for equal time in science classes; the US 6th Court of Appeals blocked the effort. The International Council on Biblical Inerrancy published a statement that scientific hypotheses about the Earth's history could not overturn scriptural teachings on creation and the flood.

Creationists who dug in where they were populated a Young Earth Creationism fashion; but an Old Earth Creationism, a version that granted the Earth's age but insisted on its divine origins, had also sprung up.

In the Eighties, the US Supreme Court ruled in Edwards v. Aguillard that equal-time practices pushing creationism alongside evolution in classrooms was unconstitutional because it illegally advanced a particular religion, ignoring the fact that other religions offer differing creation myths – and that if one religion's version could reasonably taught alongside evolution, they all could. In the process, it established a legal definition of science, explicitly ruling that "creation science" wasn't.

The Eighties also saw the rise of "intelligent design", a backdoor effort to hang in the public discourse through the argument that science could not preclude the existence of an intelligence behind the universe, evident in its order. Many Creationists went all-in on intelligent design – from a debate standpoint, anyway – changing their rhetoric to keep their elbows in the door.

On it went, into the 21st century, when the US Congress, in passing the No Child Left Behind Act, issued the Santorum Amendment – authored by law professor Phillip Johnson, who co-founded intelligent design – which stated that in the teaching of science, areas of "controversy" should be approached by educators with openness to multiple points of view.

Emboldened, Ohio adopted new standards that were intelligent-design-friendly, only to have them overturned two years later with the rejection of those standards when it came out that they had been implemented over the objections of the Ohio Department of Education.

In 2005, Kansas held court-style hearings featuring intelligent design advocates, eschewing mainstream scientists. The Republican-dominated education board then implemented lesson plans critical of evolution – leveraging the let's-cast-doubt-on-it approach, making evolution appear uncertain in young minds. The protests of the State Board Science Hearing Committee were ignored, leading to the ouster of the education board's conservative board members in 2007.

Also in 2005, the US District Court in Pennsylvania ruled in Kitzmiller v. Dover Area School District that intelligent design was a religious teaching, not a scientific one, and therefore in violation of the First Amendment.

It would be encouraging to be able to say that we've come a long way since then – but, alas, the gains have been incremental at best, and the conflict has been exacerbated by the Religious Right's increasing hunger for political power over the past two decades.

Florida has been, in recent years, the pacesetter in this area. Its Republican Governor Ron DeSantis picked all kinds of fights in the name of religion in public schools before his failed presidential run – signing, for instance, a 2021 law requiring public school students to pray or meditate for one minute every day. His Civics Literacy Excellence Initiative, aimed at turning students into "virtuous citizens", was a Christian/conservative ideology primer, raised alarms with Florida high school teachers, who found it "alarming" and "concerning". Simultaneously, DeSantis has labored hard to limit what educators from the K-12 to state college level can say in classrooms about race, gender identity, and history.

DeSantis has campaigned on the accusation that the "woke left" is a threat to public education, creating deepening divisions; and during his presidential campaign, he pledged to sign an executive order "on Day

One" that would provide religious schools with the same funding private schools receive.

DeSantis is, of course, simply the Flavor of the Month in the ongoing push by religious indoctrinators to keep their rhetoric alive, keeping long-settled debates open, and maintain the Religious Right as a political and cultural force through division and polarization. There are thousands like him, at the local, state, and federal levels, all working tirelessly to push the world back to 1925.

It's never been about "faith"; it's always about power. And in the Woke future, power is far more evenly distributed and responsibly governed. That's the ball to keep an eye on.

Forced Relocation

Forced relocations have been happening for hundreds of thousands of years, as long as humans have walked the Earth. Most, of course, have been motivated by nature – climate shifts, natural disasters, depleted resources. Since the dawn of the concept of property, which accompanied the advent of agriculture, there have also been forced relocations driven by humans themselves: one group pushing another group from one bit of land to the next. The motivations in the second case are as numerous and diverse as those in the first: the desire to possess the land; the desire to possess something the land contains; enmity between the groups; religious motivations.

Forced relocation is America's original sin, displayed in two tragic forms: the genocide of Native Americans and the acquisition of slaves from Africa. Historians might be hard-pressed to find another nation who can surpass America, in terms of sheer numbers, in this domain.

The Trail of Tears, a 20-year effort by the US government to relocate five Native American tribes from the Southeastern states to territory west of the Mississippi River, is emblematic of the former. Tens of thousands of Cherokee, Muscogee, Seminole, Chickasaw and Choctaw natives were marched west, forced from their ancestral lands – largely as an ethnic cleansing exercise, but mostly to simplify economic expansion efforts of white men. Some of those efforts were particularly avaricious, as in the removal of Cherokee from land in Georgia where large gold deposits had been discovered. This pattern repeated throughout the 19th century. Thousands of Native Americans died of disease, malnutrition and exposure on these long marches.

Far more lives were lost during the removal of Africans from their homelands to be forced into slavery. Of the 20 million who were taken, almost half never made it to America alive, dying on the march to the cost or en route across the ocean.

The US is not alone, of course, in the removal of people from their homes for horrific purposes. World War II was fought in large part because the Nazis were taking German Jews from their homes and forcing them into camps, from which millions never returned. The Soviet Union, likewise, forced segregation by ethnicity repeatedly, resettling "enemy classes" including (but not limited to) Scandinavians, Germans, Chinese, and Koreans, in a program internally referred to as "depeasantation". The Catholic Church was certainly not sinless, banishing all Protestants from Salzburg.

Resistance to the practice of forced relocation is international in scope and has persisted for the past century. The Geneva Convention, for instance, emphatically forbids it; the Rome Statute of the

International Criminal Court defines it as a crime. Criminal convictions were delivered during the Nuremberg Trials against German officials who had forced the displacement of civilian populations.

More recently, in 2023, the International Criminal Court issued warrants for the arrest of Vladimir Putin and some of his officials for the deportation of children from occupied Ukraine, in connection with Russia's invasion of that country.

It is gratifying, of course, that there is such broad global energy in support of such a moral imperative. On the other hand – tuning into this issue's 'woke' factor – intolerance of those of other ethnicities is on the rise in the US.

The surge in bigotry among white Americans in recent years can be, and has been, tied to an intensification of right-wing rhetoric designed to inflame it. A study by Clemson political scientist Steven Miller and Nicholas Davis of Texas A&M, "White Outgroup Intolerance and Declining Support for American Democracy", found that white-right intolerance and support for authoritarian rule are strongly correlated. Put another way, when white-right Americans see marginalized people benefiting from democracy, they drop their support for democracy.

This inspires authoritarians to intensify the rhetoric, as Donald Trump has done for years now, calling Mexicans "rapists" to stir up his base and amplify their fear and hatred of non-whites. And that, in turn, intensifies the political right's clamor for the deportation of as many as possible. At this writing, Trump is securing renomination by the GOP for the 2024 presidential contest, and is promising that if he returns to power, mass deportation of undocumented immigrants is at the top of his agenda, based on his fear-inducing claims that those migrants are spraying diseases every which way.

The problem is essentially that produced by the intolerance of white-right America; it is based on fears induced for *political* purposes. In all these cases, people are being removed against their will because someone in power wants something their presence is blocking.

The Woke response to this, of course, is to refuse a moral compromise (the problem of moral compromise is coming up soon, below). UNICEF offers some suggestions about how to go about this:

- *Celebrate other cultures.* Participate in social groups and community activities that are ethnically diverse. It there aren't any, start one.
- *Call out bigotry and hate speech.* When bigotry and ethnic hate are verbalized by others, disagree; when they surface in the media, publicly object, if possible.
- *Teach your children well.* Pass along attitudes of tolerance and respect to the next generation at every opportunity.
- *Act in solidarity.* Bigots are bullies. When you see someone attacked, verbally or otherwise, stand against them, even if only as a witness.
- *Support groups that promote human rights.* Get behind any group that's pushing back against bigotry and ethnic hatred.

All of these are easier said than done, of course. On the other hand, nothing is easier than going along with the crowd or uttering words you shouldn't. Naturally, doing the right thing takes more effort. But that's something we must readily accept, if we're going to reach the stars.

Sources / Recommended Reading

2001: A Space Odyssey, Arthur C. Clarke. New American Library, 1968.

The Age of Empathy: Nature's Lessons for a Kinder Society, Frans de Waal. Crown, 2009.

Anatomy of Love, Helen Fisher. W.W. & Company, 2016.

The Astonishing Hypothesis: The Scientific Search for the Soul, Francis Crick. Touchstone, 1995.

The Better Angels of Our Nature: Why Violence Has Declined, Steven Pinker. Viking, 2011.

The Biology of Moral Systems, Richard D. Alexander. Aldine Transaction, 1987.

Chasing the Enterprise: Achieving Star Trek's Vision of the Human Future, Scott Robinson. Paleos Media, 2020.

The Children of Babel: Essays on the Inherent Nature of Artificial Intelligence and Consciousness, Scott Robinson. Paleos Media, 2020.

A Companion to Cognitive Science (Blackwell Companions to Philosophy), ed. William Bechtel and George Graham. Wiley-Blackwell, 1998.

A Companion to the Philosophy of Mind (Blackwell Companions to Philosophy), ed. Samuel Guttenplan. John Wiley & Sons, 1996.

The Conscious Mind: In Search of a Fundamental Theory, David Chalmers. Oxford University Press, 1997).

Consciousness and Language, John Searle. Cambridge University Press, 2002.

Consciousness Explained, Daniel Dennett. Back Bay Books, 1992.

Contact, Carl Sagan. Simon & Schuster, 1985.

A Cooperative Species: Human Reciprocity and Its Evolution, Samuel Bowles & Herbert Gintis. Princeton University Press, 2011.

The Creation of Inequality, Kent Flannery, Joyce Marcus. Harvard University Press, 2012.

Darwin's Dangerous Idea, Daniel Dennett. Simon & Schuster, 1996.

Demonic Males, Richard Wrangham and Dale Peterson. Mariner Books, 1997.

The End of War, John Horgan. McSweeney's Books, 2012.

The Engine of Reason, The Seat of the Soul: A Philosophical Journey into the Brain, Paul Churchland. MIT Press, 1995.

The Evolution of Cooperation, Robert Axelrod. Basic Books, 2006.

The Evolution of Morality, Richard Joyce. MIT Press, 2006.

Evolutionary Origins of Morality: Cross-Disciplinary Perspectives, Leonard D. Katz (ed.). Imprint Academic, 2002.

Fantasia Mathematica, Clifton Fadiman, ed. Copernicus, 1997.

Fluid Concepts and Creative Analogies: Computer Models of the Fundamental Mechanisms of Thought, Douglas Hofstadter. Basic Books, 1996.

Genesis: The Deep Origins of Society, E.O. Wilson. Liveright, 2019.

Gödel, Escher, Bach: An Eternal Golden Braid, Douglas Hofstadter. Basic Books (anniversary edition), 1999.

HAL 9000: An Unauthorized Biography, Scott Robinson, Paleos Media, 2020.

HAL's Legacy: 2001's Computer as Dream and Reality, ed. David G. Stork. MIT Press, 1997.

Hierarchy in the Forest: The Evolution of Egalitarian Behavior, Christopher Boehm. Harvard University Press, 2001.

The Human Potential for Peace: An Anthropological Challenge to Assumptions About War and Violence, Douglas Fry. Oxford University Press, 2006.

I Am a Strange Loop, Douglas Hofstadter. Basic Books, 2007.

I Think I'm Right in Saying That? Scott Robinson. Paleos Media, 2019.

Infinity and the Mind: The Science and Philosophy of the Infinite, Rudy Rucker. Birkhauser, 1982.

The Intentional Stance, Daniel Dennett. Bradford Books, 1989.

Intentionality, John Searle. Cambridge University Press, 1983.

Intuition Pumps and Other Tools for Thinking, Daniel Dennett. W.W. Norton & Company, 2014.

Labyrinths, Jorge Luis Borges. New Directions, 2007.

Le Ton Beau de Marot: In Praise of the Music of Language, Douglas Hofstadter. Basic Books, 1997

Less Than Human: Why We Demean, Enslave, and Exterminate Others. St. Martin's Press, 2011.

Macmillan Dictionary of Psychology, Stuart Sutherland. Palgrave MacMillan, 1991.

Mappings in Thought and Language, Gilles Fauconnier. Cambridge University Press, 1997.

The Master and His Emissary, Iain McGilchrist. Yale University Press, 2019.

The Meaning of Human Existence, Edward O. Wilson. Liveright, 2015.

Metaphysics, Richard Taylor. Prentiss-Hall, 1992.

Mind-Body Problems: Science, Subjectivity & Who We Really Are, John Horgan. Knot Press, 2019.

The Mind's I: Fantasies and Reflections on Self and Soul, Douglas Hofstadter, Daniel Dennett. Basic Books, 1981.

Minds, Brains and Science, John Searle. Harvard University Press, 1984.

The Moral Animal: Why We Are the Way We Are, Robert Wright. Vintage Books, 1994.

The Moral Molecule, Paul J. Zak. Transworld Publishers, 2013.

Moral Origins: The Evolution of Virtue, Altruism, and Shame, Christopher Boehm. Basic Books, 2012.

The Most Dangerous Animal: Human Nature and the Origins of War, David Livingstone Smith. St. Martin's Griffin, 2007.

The Mystery of Consciousness, John Searle. The New York Review of Books, 1997.
A Natural History of Human Morality, Michael Tomasello. Harvard University Press, 2016.

A Natural History of Peace, ed. Thomas Gregor. Vanderbilt University Press, 1996.

Neuroscience and Philosophy: Brain, Mind, and Language, Daniel Robinson et al. Columbia University Press, 2009.

The Neuroscience of Human Relationships, Louis Cozolino. W.W. Norton, 2014.

Non-Zero: The Logic of Human Destiny, Robert Wright. Vintage, 2000.

On Intelligence: How a New Understanding of the Brain Will Lead to the Creation of Truly Intelligent Machines, Jeff Hawkins and Sandra Blakeslee. St. Martin's Griffin, 2005.

Order Out of Chaos: Man's New Dialogue with Nature, Ilya Prigogine and Isabelle Stengers. William Heinemann Ltd., 1984.

Organization of Behavior: A Neuropsychological Theory, Donald Hebb. Wiley, 1949.

Origin, Dan Brown. Transworld Publishers, 2018.

The Origins of Virtue: Human Instincts and the Evolution of Cooperation, Matt Ridley. Penguin Books, 1998.

Prehistory: The Making of the Human Mind, Colin Renfrew. Modern Library, 2007.

Quiddities: An Intermittently Philosophical Dictionary, W.V. Quine. Belknap Press, 1989.

Routledge Encyclopedia of Philosophy, ed. Edward Craig. Routledge, 1998.

The Selfish Gene, Richard Dawkins. Oxford University Press, 1989.

Social: Why Our Brains Are Wired to Connect, Matthew D. Leiberman. Broadway Books, 2013.

Sociobiology, Edward O. Wilson. Belknap Press, 2000 (25th anniversary edition).

Star Trek and Humanism, Scott Robinson. Paleos Media, 2023.

Star Trek Thought Experiments, Scott Robinson. Paleos Media, 2022.

Survival of the Nicest: How Altruism Made Us Human and Why It Pays to Get Along, Stefan Klein. The Experiment, 2014.

Trekonomics: The Economics of Star Trek, Manu Saadia. Pipertext, 2016.

The Triumph of Sociobiology, John Alcock. Oxford University Press, 2001.

Unto Others: The Evolution and Psychology of Unselfish Behavior, Elliott Sober and David Sloan Wilson. Harvard University Press, 1998.

Us Against Them: How Tribalism Affects the Way We Think, Bruce Rozenblit. Transcendent Publications, 2008.

Views of the Chinese Room: New Essays on Searle and Artificial Intelligence, ed. John Preston and Mark Bishop. Clarendon Press, 2002.

War, Peace, and Human Nature, Douglas Fry (ed.). Oxford University Press, 2013.

Why We Cooperate, Michael Tomasello, et al. MIT Press, 2009.

The World until Yesterday, Jared Diamond. Penguin Books, 2012.

Internet sources

https://www.pbs.org/newshour/nation/annual-report-shows-systemic-racism-continues-to-bring-down-black-peoples-quality-of-life

https://www.hsph.harvard.edu/magazine/magazine_article/discrimination-in-america/

https://www.un.org/en/about-us/universal-declaration-of-human-rights

https://www.pewresearch.org/social-trends/2019/04/09/race-in-america-2019/

https://opseu.org/wp-content/uploads/2018/12/30_basic_human_rights_list_english.pdf

https://www.pewresearch.org/politics/2006/01/05/strong-public-support-for-right-to-die/

https://www.ptsd.va.gov/understand/common/common_adults.asp#:~:text=About%206%20out%20of%20every,if%20their%20symptoms%20go%20away.

https://hr.nih.gov/working-nih/civil/post-traumatic-stress-disorder-ptsd-2023

https://www.ptsd.va.gov/understand/common/common_veterans.asp#:~:text=At%20some%20point%20in%20their,of%20100%2C%20or%206%25

About the Author

Scott Robinson is a journalist, social scientist, public speaker and musician, and was for 20 years a music critic with the *Louisville Courier-Journal*. He is also a member of the Scottish Society of Louisville. He has also been published in *Rolling Stone* and *The Wall Street Journal*. He can be reached at

scott.robinson@glenmillscience.com